Police Research Series
Paper 140

Risk Assessment and Management of Known Sexual and Violent Offenders: A review of current issues

Hazel Kemshall

"The views expressed in this report are those of the authors, not necessarily those of the Home Office (nor do they reflect Government policy)."

Editor: Lawrence Singer
Home Office
Policing and Reducing Crime Unit
Research, Development and Statistics Directorate
Clive House, Petty France
London, SW1H 9HD

Policing and Reducing Crime Unit: Police Research Series

The Policing and Reducing Crime Unit (PRC Unit) is part of the Research, Development and Statistics Directorate of the Home Office. The PRC Unit carries out and commissions research in the social and management sciences on policing and crime reduction.

The Police Research Series presents research material on crime prevention and detection as well as police management and organisation issues.

ISBN 1-84082-601-0

Copies of this publication can be made available in formats accessible to the visually impaired on request.

Foreword

Public Protection Panels (PPPs) now play an important role in the process of assessing and managing sexual and violent offenders in the community. Decisions made by these panels are informed by information from a range of risk assessment methods. This PRC report provides an overview of the different means of risk assessment and management for such offenders. The management and operation of multi-agency PPPs has been explored in detail in a complementary study, *Risk Management of Sexual and Violent Offenders: The work of Public Protection Panels* (Maguire et al, 2001). Within a fast-changing field, this report is intended to provide practitioners with a snapshot of the risk assessment tools currently available. It will be of interest to all those in the police service and beyond involved in the practice of managing sexual and violent offenders in the community.

Carole F. Willis
Head of Policing and Reducing Crime Unit
Research, Development and Statistics Directorate
Home Office
April 2001

Acknowledgements

Professor Grubin's literature review (1998) provided an important starting point for this work. Professor Mike Maguire and Lesley Noaks of Cardiff University provided comments on the first draft, and my thanks are extended to Gay Hill and the staff of the West Midlands Probation Service library for provision of much of the literature. Staff at the Scraptoft library, De Montfort University, also provided immense support and Ann Lane provided invaluable advice and support with the final layout of the report. Finally, I would like to acknowledge Emma Marshall of PRC. Her support and encouragement ensured that the report reached publication.

Much of the thinking and knowledge used in the preparation of this report was acquired during research sponsored by the Economic and Social Research Council, entitled 'Risk in Probation Practice' (1994-1997; L211252018)

The author

Hazel Kemshall is Professor of Community and Criminal Justice in the Department of Social and Community Studies at De Montfort University.

PRC would like to thank Professor Sylvia Walby of the University of Leeds and Professor Don Grubin of the Department of Forensic Psychiatry, St. Nicholas Hospital, Newcastle-Upon-Tyne, who acted as external assessors for this report.

Executive summary

This report reviews the literature relating to the assessment and management of sex offenders, serious violent offenders, and those deemed to be 'dangerous'[1] and therefore requiring special measures. It has been produced to help those in the police, probation service and other agencies who play an active part in multi-agency public protection panel meetings and have responsibility for risk assessment and risk management. The report covers four broad areas:

[1] The terms 'dangerous offender' and 'dangerousness' used throughout this report are based upon the definition of dangerousness offered by the Butler Committee 1975.

- the legislative provisions covering sexual offenders, and specifically those sexual and violent offenders deemed to be dangerous;

- different approaches to risk assessment;

- the current tools available in this area; and,

- risk management.

A complementary PRC study, *Risk Management of Sexual and Violent Offenders: The work of the Public Protection Panels* (Maguire, Kemshall, Noaks and Wincup, 2001) examines the practices of multi-agency public protection panels. In particular, it considers the range of working practices to assess and manage risk across several police areas and identifies good practice.

Legislative provisions

The recent legislative provisions to manage sexual offenders in the community (i.e. the Sex Offenders Act 1997, the Crime [Sentences] Act 1997, the use of Sex Offender Orders under the Crime and Disorder Act 1998, and a package of measures within the Criminal Justice and Court Services Act 2000) place clear responsibilities on to police personnel. Those responsibilities include the risk assessment and registration of sex offenders, the effective assessment and communication of risk with other relevant agencies and the management of offenders in the community. Serious violent offenders, and those who are seen as presenting a serious risk of harm to the public, have also been subject to legislative changes to increase public protection. Most notable amongst these new arrangements is the Crime and Disorder Act 1998, which provides for periods of extended supervision at the end of a custodial sentence where the court considers that an extended licence is required to prevent further offending upon release. For violent offenders, custodial penalties must be longer than four years and the period of extension of licence cannot exceed five years. The Crime (Sentences) Act 1997 also introduced mandatory sentencing for certain categories of violent crime (e.g. grievous bodily harm with intent, wounding, manslaughter, and incitement to murder).

Finally, a range of measures designed to strengthen the protection of children were incorporated within the Criminal Justice and Court Services Act 2000. These included the creation of a statutory duty on the police and probation services to jointly establish arrangements for assessing and managing the risks posed by sexual and violent offenders in the community.

Approaches to risk assessment

In order to assess and manage risk effectively, reliable methods are necessary. There are two basic approaches: the clinical and the actuarial.

- *Clinical methods* are essentially a diagnostic assessment derived in part from the medical and mental health fields.

Although the clinical method is considered less reliable than the actuarial method, it can provide important information on individual risky behaviours, stresses related to environmental factors, and assist in establishing appropriate treatment and risk management plans. Recent research has begun to confirm the significant role that structured clinical judgement, particularly in the form of structured behavioural rating scales, can play as part of actuarially-based tools.

- *Actuarial methods* utilise statistical techniques to generate risk predictors.

Although actuarial methods have a greater track record for accuracy, they do, however, have a number of limitations and can be used inappropriately. It is important to recognise that there are limits to a technique that uses information generalised from a population for application to an individual under assessment. The use of meta-analyses – research based on the analysis of a large number of primary studies – to develop risk predictors can result in overly simplistic outcomes which fail to capture the complexity of the processes involved. A further problem relates to the predictions of risk where there is a low incidence of risky behaviours in the population as a whole.

The combined use of clinical and actuarial methods in an holistic approach to risk assessment is now advocated as the approach most likely to enhance both the predictive accuracy and usefulness of risk assessments for sexual and dangerous offenders.

Risk assessment tools

There are two basic methods for predicting sex offence recidivism: the 'Rapid Risk Assessment for Sex Offence Recidivism' (RRASOR) and the 'Structured Anchored

Clinical Judgement' (SACJ). Both predict well. They have been combined into a single tool – STATIC 99 – and this has led to a modest increase in predictive accuracy for recidivism. Most recently, SACJ has been updated and refined into MATRIX 2000, and this has been quickly adopted for sex offender risk assessment in the UK. None of these tools predict seriousness or likely harm and they are not advocated as stand-alone tools.

The various tools used to assess *violent* offenders are also reviewed in this study. Because violent offenders are not a homogenous group, tools have been developed for different types of violent offenders, in a range of settings and for differing offences. This makes comparability of different tools difficult and inhibits transferability of assessment tools across offender populations. Those tools which are likely to be of most use to personnel engaged in multi-agency public protection work have been examined most closely. Of these, the Violence Risk Assessment Guide (VRAG) is the most accurate and the most widely used. The structured clinical assessment tool, HCR-20, provides additional value in terms of identifying those dynamic factors requiring case intervention and treatment. Recent developments in assessment which combine multi-factoral analyses and classification tree approaches are also briefly reviewed, although presently they have not been fully evaluated.

Risk management

Risk management is an area where the activities of the police service and other relevant agencies such as the probation service are often measured harshly in the light of serious incidents and harm to victims. The report reviews current literature on effective interventions for sexual and violent offenders. While early evaluations of the effectiveness of treatment for sex offenders tended to be pessimistic, evaluations of treatment programmes throughout the 1990s have been more positive. These more recent evaluations suggest that cognitive-behavioural approaches are the most promising, although some offenders (such as those engaged in violent penetrative sex offending) are less amenable to treatment. The integrity of treatment programmes and the accurate targeting of high-risk offenders are also seen as key features of effective treatment. Motivation to change on the part of the offender and the timing of treatment are also crucial to success.

There have been very few systematic evaluations of violent offender treatment programmes. Assessing the impact and effectiveness of such treatment programmes is further hindered by the varied nature of violent offences and violent offender groups entering specific programmes. However, evidence to date clearly suggests that cognitive-behavioural programmes such as the Vermont Cognitive Self Change programme are effective. The Vermont programme recognises that the promotion of an offender's internal controls needs to be balanced with the implementation of external controls. Key features of the system are mechanisms for early response to signs of relapse (such as failure to attend appointments) and systematic monitoring of progress. Furthermore, treatment interventions are integrated into a broader risk management strategy, to ensure monitoring, surveillance, and appropriate actions to enforce conditions and controls on participants as appropriate.

In a climate of increasing public scrutiny and concern for accountability, the reliable assessment and effective management of sexual and violent offenders is a pressing issue. This report distils and reviews the most relevant literature and demonstrates its relevance to the roles and responsibilities of police and probation personnel assessing and managing risk from known sexual and violent offenders.

Contents

List of figures

1. Introduction

Background

The incidence and subsequent harm resulting from sex offending, particularly paedophilia, is now undisputed (Grubin, 1998). A survey of 21 countries, including Canada and the United States, has established the existence of widespread child sexual abuse (Finkelhor, 1994). In England and Wales, Home Office statistics have established that males and females aged 10 to 15 are most at risk of indecent assault 'with 66 male victimisations and 327 female victimisations per 100,000 population' (Home Office, 1998a: 19). The physical and psychological harm caused by sexual offending is also well documented (Grubin, 1998; Scottish Office Social Work Inspectorate, 1997), with impacts ranging from minimal physical harm, to extensive abuse and psychological trauma.

Dangerous offenders, defined as those likely to inflict serious physical or psychological harm on others (Butler Committee, 1975), have also been the subject of concern among both policy makers and the public. In particular, those offenders who harm vulnerable persons (e.g. children or the elderly), or for whom surveillance after release from prison or from a mental hospital has broken down (Blom-Cooper et al, 1995) have attracted attention. Offences committed by these people may involve physical violence or the threat of violence (e.g. 'stalking'), and can have significant psychological effects on the victims. The range of offences and offenders that can now be considered 'potentially dangerous' is extensive.

The concept of the dangerous offender or the 'potentially dangerous offender' is not new (for example, see Bottoms [1977] and Floud and Young [1981] for a review of the debate around dangerous offenders in the 1970s). Its use has been subject to much criticism partly on the grounds of imprecision, but also the lack of accuracy in the assessment tools used to assess potentially dangerous offenders, and ethical issues arising from false positive predictions (Floud and Young 1981). Despite such early cautions over the use of the term and its implications for legislation, the 1980s and 1990s have seen an increased use of the concept of dangerousness in penal policy.

Both violent and sex offenders can be dangerous and may share some of the characteristics that define how and why they are dangerous (for example, in terms of the physical harm or psychological trauma inflicted on victims). However, the diversity of offender types and offences committed makes the presentation of them as a homogeneous group difficult. Indeed, recent legislation has increasingly defined sex offenders as a distinct group requiring different responses (i.e. registration). Therefore, for the purposes of this report violent and sex offenders are treated as two different groups.

Scope and purpose of the report

This study is intended as a practical document focusing on those risk assessment tools most likely to assist personnel engaged in public protection panel work. It draws upon the research literature from both the UK and USA, but is necessarily selective rather than exhaustive. The primary focus of multi-agency risk public protection panels is convicted and registered sex offenders, and those known offenders who present a significant risk of harm to the public and are considered 'potentially dangerous' (Maguire et al, 2001). Their offending may be against either adults or children, although panels are most often concerned with the assessment and management of predatory paedophiles and serious violent offenders post custody or as subjects of community orders. This remit has necessarily informed the scope of this review; some offence, types such as domestic violence and familial violence against children have generally been excluded from this study as they are usually addressed by other multi-agency mechanisms, for example domestic violence units and child protection case conferences.

At this early stage, it is important to acknowledge the inherent difficulties around relying largely upon studies of predominantly white, male and convicted offender populations. Such studies do not necessarily reflect the volume or frequency of the activities in the population as a whole. Nor should we lose sight of the fact that *reconviction* does not equate with actual *re-offending*. The limitations that this impose have been well documented (see for instance, Lloyd, Mair and Hough, 1994).

It is hoped that this report will assist both police and probation personnel in their risk assessment and management tasks both at time of registration (for sex offenders) and in their multi-agency public protection panel work. Furthermore, since risk assessment and risk management is increasingly a multi-agency, corporate endeavour, it is anticipated that staff in other agencies, such as health, social services and housing, are likely to find the report of use.

Specifically, the report aims to present an overview of:

● the key issues in risk assessment and the broad approaches currently adopted;

● the current risk assessment tools for sexual and violent offenders;

● the principles of risk management; and,

● risk management interventions for these categories of offenders.

This field continues to develop rapidly, particularly in respect of assessment tools, and, where appropriate, brief reference is made to current developments, such as the OASys prison-probation assessment tool (although full evaluation of such tools may be some way off).

Structure of the report

Section 2 outlines legislative provisions for both sex offenders and violent offenders, as well as roles and responsibilities in risk assessment. Section 3 discusses definitions of risk, and focuses on the principal approaches that are used to assess risk (clinical versus actuarial methods). It also highlights those 'dynamic' risk factors most likely to assist personnel in their public protection work and the key problems with risk assessment. Section 4 gives an overview of available risk assessment tools for sex offenders and violent offenders. Section 5 deals with the issue of risk management, while section 6 concludes the report, summarising briefly the main issues involved in the area of risk assessment and risk management.

2. Legislative provisions, roles and responsibilities

This section briefly reviews the legislative provisions in respect of sex and violent offenders, the background and key aims of the legislation, and the practical implications of the legislation, particularly for police personnel.

Background

The 1990s witnessed a growing preoccupation around public protection, with policy and subsequent legislation shaped by two separate, although often overlapping, imperatives:

- the protection of the public from the risk of serious harm, usually expressed as serious physical and psychological harm arising from violent offenders; and,

- the desire to respond more effectively to the growing risk presented by paedophiles and the increase in child sexual abuse (Grubin, 1998).

Both concerns have given rise to legislative change and policy initiatives that have directly impacted upon the work of police and probation services. The key aims of legislation have been:

- the extended use of custody for dangerous offenders and in particular the use of preventative sentencing and selective incapacitation on the grounds of risk (Feeley and Simon, 1994); and,

- extended monitoring and surveillance of sexual offenders in the community and upon release from prison, including the use of registers and 'tracking' systems (Hebenton and Thomas, 1996a, 1996b, 1997).

Specific legislative change has been paralleled by the development of policies and tools to identify and assess risky offenders. During the 1990s such changes have been evident within the probation service and more recently, the police service, as it has become concerned over the effective implementation of sex offender registration. Furthermore, as a result of the need to engage with public protection, multi-agency co-operation has formalised into the development of 'Public Protection Panels' with the remit to assess and manage potentially dangerous offenders and reduce risk to the public. In practice such panels not only exchange information on offenders, but also engage in formalised risk assessments and management planning. Whilst convicted sexual and violent offenders are most frequently considered by the panels, in some areas the remit has been extended to include potentially dangerous but unconvicted offenders who are on bail, and known offenders who are not the subject of statutory supervision (Maguire et al, 2001). The Criminal Justice and Court Services Act 2000 placed a statutory duty jointly upon the police and probation services to establish arrangements for assessing and managing the risks posed by all sex offenders and other dangerous offenders released into the community[1] (Home Office, 2000).

Whilst the registration of sex offenders under the Sex Offenders Act 1997 is formally the responsibility of the police, Home Office Circular 39/97 encourages police and probation to liaise closely over risk assessment, and co-operate with other agencies in the interests of effective risk management. In practice this has resulted in a varied approach to registered sex offenders, with some police areas choosing to assess formally all registered sex offenders at public protection panels, and others referring only individual cases where risk to the public is considered to be high (Maguire et al, 2001).

Provisions for sex offenders

Sex offenders (and to a lesser extent, violent offenders) have been identified as requiring special provision within the criminal justice system. The Criminal Justice Act (1991) included provisions for preventative sentencing[2] and extended supervision[3], and more recently the Sex Offenders Act 1997 established arrangements for a Sex Offender Register designed to monitor and track such offenders (see Plotnikoff and Woolfson, 2000). The Act requires offenders to notify the police of their name and address within a specified time period and applies to all those convicted of, or cautioned for, an offence listed in Schedule 1. The offences triggering a duty to register and the relevant registration periods are summarised in Figure 1.

The consultation paper 'Community Protection Order' (Home Office, 1997a) noted, however, that approximately 100,000 sex offenders cautioned or convicted prior to the implementation of the Act on 1 September 1997 were not covered by these registration arrangements (Power, 1999). This left a significant group outside the remit of registration procedures. In addition, commentators such as Bean (1997) and Cobley (1997), noted that registration in itself could not deliver child protection; such protection can only be achieved through effective risk management plans and their competent implementation. Partly in response to these concerns, the Government introduced the Sex Offender Order under the Crime and Disorder Act 1998. These Orders came into force on 1 December 1998, and the conditions are summarised in Figure 2.

[1] *New measures in the Criminal Justice and Court Services Act 2000 also placed a statutory duty on the probation service to find out if a victim wishes to be informed about the release arrangements of any offender serving 12 months or more for a sexual or violent offence, and if so to consult and notify the victim about those release arrangements.*

[2] *Enacted under Section 2 (2) b.*
[3] *Enacted under Section 44.*

Figure 1: Registration requirements under the Sex Offenders Act 1997

Offences:

- unlawful intercourse with a girl under 13, and if the defendant is aged 20 or over, with a girl between 13 and 16;
- causing or encouraging sexual intercourse with, or indecent assault on, or the prostitution of, a girl under 16;
- inciting a girl under 16 to incestuous sexual intercourse;
- indecency with a child under 14;
- incest by a man with a victim under 18;
- rape;
- indecent assault on a man or woman (except where sentence is less than 30 months and the victim is over 18);
- buggery and gross indecency where defendant is aged 20 or over and the victim is under 18;
- crimes relating to child pornography; and,
- assault with intent to commit buggery with a victim under 18.

Registration requirements:

- to notify the police of name, address, and date of birth within 14 days of caution/conviction/release/sentence;
- to notify the police of any change in the above;
- to notify the police of any 14 day period away from this address (continuous or aggregated over 12 months);
- any unreasonable failure to comply with the registration requirements or the deliberate provision of false information is a summary crime; and,
- deliberate provision of false information is a summary crime.

Registration periods:

- if the offender receives a caution or is given a non-custodial sentence, the registration period is five years;
- if the offender receives a sentence under six months custody, the registration period is seven years;
- if the offender receives a sentence of six to 30 months custody, the registration period is 10 years;
- if the offender receives a sentence of 30 plus months, the registration period is indefinite; and,

(from Cobley, 1997; Hebenton and Thomas, 1997; Power, 1998; Sex Offenders Act 1997, Schedule 1 and Section 51)

Figure 2: Provisions for Sex Offender Orders

- a Sex Offender Order is available to a chief officer of police from a magistrates' court if there is reasonable cause to believe that the defendant 'has acted' in such a way that an order is necessary to protect the public from the offender;

- negative conditions or 'prohibitions' can be attached to the Orders as thought necessary to achieve protection of the public, (e.g. restricting access to potential victims, or access to particular places);

- an offender subject to an Order has to register under the Sex Offenders Act 1997 within 14 days of the order being made (this allows for retrospective registration of offenders);

- Orders run for a minimum of five years;

- offenders can appeal to the Crown Court against the Order being made, and to a magistrates' court for variation or discharge; and,

- breach of a Sex Offender Order can carry up to a five-year custodial penalty upon indictment.

(from Cobley, 1997; Power, 1998)

Sex Offender Orders are civil orders requiring civil standards of proof but carrying a criminal penalty if breached (Power, 1998)[4]. An important feature of the Act is that it introduces negative or prohibitive conditions to control the behaviour of sex offenders[5].

In September 2000, the government announced its intentions to make a number of amendments to the Sex Offenders Act 1997. These included giving a new power for the Crown Court regarding placing of restrictions on offenders covered by the Act to have immediate effect on release from custody (e.g. requirements around not approaching victims). Changes were also announced regarding the registration provisions of the Act (the requirement to notify foreign travel, increasing the penalty for non-registration, additional powers regarding the provision of photographs and fingerprints, and a shortening of the period for initial registration to 72 hours). The amendments were incorporated into the Criminal Justice and Court Services Act 2000 (Home Office, 2000).

Provisions for dangerous offenders

Dangerous offenders have also attracted the concerns of policy makers. The Criminal Justice Act (1991)[6] allowed for the imposition of a custodial sentence on the grounds of 'serious harm' to the public and for non-commensurate sentencing on the grounds of preventing future 'serious harm' by the offender[7]. The Crime

[4] *Breach of a Sex Offender Order can carry up to a five year custodial penalty upon indictment.*

[5] *Offenders can only be required not to do something – for example, offenders might be required not to visit a certain area, or not to speak to certain people.*

[6] *Under Section 1 (2) (b).*

[7] *Section 2 (2) (b).*

(Sentences) Act 1997 also gave legislative expression to a number of public protection concerns expressed in the White Paper *Protecting the Public* (Home Office, 1996), and extended the sentencing powers available on the grounds of seriousness. Section 2 of this Act allows for mandatory life imprisonment when convicted for a second time for certain serious violent/sexual offences. These are outlined in Figure 3.

Figure 3: Offences attracting a mandatory life sentence when committed a second time

- attempting, conspiring or inciting to commit murder or soliciting murder;

- manslaughter;

- wounding or causing grievous bodily harm with intent[8];

- rape or attempt to commit rape;

- intercourse with a girl under 13;

- possession of a firearm with intent to injure, use of a firearm to resist arrest, or carrying a firearm with criminal intent[9]; and,

- robbery where during the commission of the offence the defendant had in his/her possession a firearm or imitation firearm within the meaning of the Firearms Act 1968.

(from Teggin, 1998)

[8] *Offences Against the Person Act 1861, s. 18.*

[9] *Firearms Act 1968, ss 16, 17, 18.*

The Crime and Disorder Act 1998 continued this protective theme within Section 58. This gives courts the power to add a period of extended post-release supervision to the sentence normally imposed upon a person convicted of a sexual or violent offence (Home Office, 1998b). These extended licences can apply to sex offenders for up to 10 years, and to violent offenders for up to five years[10]. The court may not, however, pass an extended sentence unless the custodial sentence is four years or more. Serious violent offending such as wounding with intent to cause grievous bodily harm is also punishable by the mandatory sentencing of the Crime (Sentences) Act 1997 (see Figure 3), and it is likely that courts will choose to deal with a dangerous offender in this manner (*Sentencing News*, 1998).

[10] *For a violent offender the combined period must not exceed the maximum sentence for the offence.*

The prevention of dangerous behaviours by mentally disordered persons with severe personality disorders has also received attention through proposals announced by the Home Secretary in February 1999. In the paper *Managing Dangerous People with Severe Personality Disorder*, the Home Office identified that a small group of people with severe personality disorder pose a very high risk to the public (calculated to be in the region of 2,000 people in England and Wales)(Home Office, 1999). The Home Office document categorises the 'overwhelming majority' of such persons as 'people who have committed serious offences such as murder, manslaughter, arson, serious sex offences, or grievous bodily harm' (p.9). Of the 2,000, it is estimated that between 300-600 men are at large within the community, with the equivalent figures for juveniles and women described as 'very low'. The impetus behind the proposals has been the growing recognition that people with dangerous severe personality disorders have been released from prison or hospital whilst still posing a high risk to public safety. The proposals aim to introduce preventative detention for those suffering a severe personality disorder and who pose a high risk of harm to others, but who are deemed untreatable under the Mental Health Act 1983. The proposals are particularly concerned with:

- the creation of new legislative powers for the extended detention and supervision of dangerous severe personality disordered individuals;

- identification and risk assessment based upon agreed national protocols and assessment tools; and,

- long-term case management and the development of best practice management strategies to reduce risk to the public.

Whilst beyond the scope of this report, these proposals are likely to have a limited impact upon the work of multi-agency public protection panels in those few cases where they may be required to provide information or refer individuals for specialist assessment.

Implications of legislative provisions and policy developments

The cumulative impact of the legislation reviewed here has been to identify those responsible for a wide range of serious violent offending, sex offending, and who demonstrate the potential for such offending, as offenders for whom special measures of selective incarceration or community surveillance are both required and justified. This has been reflected by increased restriction, surveillance and monitoring of such offenders in the community. Connelly and Williamson (2000) characterise this approach to sexual and violent offenders as a 'community protection model' in which legislation prioritises public protection, partly through provisions for mandatory, indeterminate and preventative sentencing.

These provisions have had important implications for the work of the police and probation services, not only in terms of the requirement to identify and assess those offenders who present a significant risk of harm to the public, but also in terms of formalised co-operation to both assess and manage these offenders. This has resulted in the development of formal protocols of multi-agency working and the development of organisational and administrative systems to share both information and decision-making.

While the Sex Offenders Act 1997 and the Crime and Disorder Act 1998 have placed new responsibilities on the police in the field of risk management, the probation service maintains a key role in risk assessment on some offenders at the point of sentence, during community supervision and at the point of release from custody. These assessments generally take two forms: assessment of the risk of re-offending and assessments of the likely harm from potentially dangerous offenders.

Risk of re-offending assessments are routinely carried out in the provision of reports to the court under the requirements of the Criminal Justice Act (1991) or during statutory supervision. These assessments use various risk of re-offending tools aimed at identifying risk factors and the likelihood of re-offending. Assessment of dangerousness is more often targeted at serious offenders within the community and those approaching release. These assessments use various structured interviewing techniques and aide memoires (see, for example, West Yorkshire Probation Service, undated), and are used to identify offenders for registration on potentially dangerous offender registers (Home Office, 1988). These cases are likely to be discussed with police at multi-agency panels, informing the assessments they are involved in and any subsequent risk management strategy.

Summary

Recent legislation has increasingly defined both sex offenders and violent offenders as distinct offender groups requiring increased levels of surveillance and control. This has resulted in distinct roles and responsibilities for police in the assessment and registration of sex offenders in particular, and also for the formalised information exchange between those agencies involved in the assessment of management of such offenders.

3. Approaches to risk assessment

Key definitions

'Risk' has traditionally been a neutral term meaning the chance of gain or the chance of loss (Parton, 1996). Increasingly, however, risk has become associated with notions of hazard, danger or harm (Douglas, 1992), and in criminal justice with the:

> *...uncertain prediction about future behaviour, with a chance that the future outcome of the behaviour will be harmful or negative*
>
> (Kemshall, 1996a: v)

A risk assessment can therefore be characterised as a:

> *...probability calculation that a harmful behaviour or event will occur, and involves an assessment about the frequency of the behaviour/event, its likely impact and who it will affect*
>
> (Kemshall, 1996a: v)

Within a risk assessment, the term 'danger' describes the actual or potential exposure to harm, or the likelihood of certain individuals or circumstances to present harm. Hence the use of the term 'dangerous' for certain individuals who present an actual or potential harm to others. Scott (1977) has, however, suggested that to be useful, any assessment of dangerousness must specify:

- the *behaviour* of concern;

- the *potential damage or harm* likely to result from that behaviour; and,

- the *probability* that it will occur and under what circumstances.

The level and impact of harm has been central to recent preventative measures (see Section 2), and harm reduction is a key principle of such legislative measures. Harm incorporates physical, sexual, violent and psychological harm. The offenders most likely to present such harm are classified by legislation, for example Section 31 (1) of the Criminal Justice Act 1991, which defines violent and sexual offences, and by subsequent legislation in the intervening period.

However, in practice, both sex offending and violent offending are difficult to define in practice and neither can be considered a homogeneous category (see Grubin, 1998 on sex offending). The 1997 Scottish Office paper, *A Commitment to Protect – Supervising Sex Offenders: Proposals for more effective practice*, concerns itself with those sexual offences that involve exploitation and/or assault. The following categories are presented as a useful starting point:

- familial child sex abusers;

- non-familial abusers;

- paedophiles;

- rapists; and,

- indecent exposers.

A different if complementary approach is offered by Grubin (1998: 14), who suggests a categorisation based upon the offender's:

- choice of victim;

- criminal background;

- sexual arousal patterns;

- social functioning; and,

- risk of re-offending.

Violent offenders are an equally diverse group, encompassing those who, *inter alia:*

- are involved in domestic violence;

- harm others in the commission of other offences (e.g. by using firearms);

- harm vulnerable persons (such as children or the elderly);

- use threat or force which is likely to result in injury to people (e.g. offences of robbery) (Megargee, 1976:12); and,

- commit violence as a result of mental disorder (Swanson and Holzer, 1990).

This diversity indicates that risk assessment tools need to be chosen on the basis of their applicability to the offender group and offence type under consideration.

Problems in risk assessment

The key issue in risk assessment is accuracy, and the avoidance of either over-prediction or under-prediction. In any risk assessment there are four possible outcomes. These are displayed in Figure 4.

Figure 4: Prediction outcomes

		Prediction	
		Yes	**No**
O U T C O M E	Yes	A True positive prediction	B False negative prediction
	No	C False positive prediction	D True negative prediction

Risk predictions can be right by predicting correctly that a harmful behaviour will occur (Box A), or by predicting correctly that a harmful behaviour will not occur (Box D). However, errors are also likely and they carry substantial costs. Box B identifies those cases in which a risk of harm is not identified but does occur, whereas Box C identifies those cases in which harm is predicted but does not occur.

In Box B cases, the consequences can be particularly severe. Victims may be harmed or killed, and workers and their agencies can be brought into disrepute. In Box C cases, the criminal justice system can be accused of over-intervening, with an impact on civil liberties and waste of precious resources. Box B cases encourage a move towards more defensive practice, caution and over-prediction amongst practitioners and their agencies as a response to costly failures. Box C cases tend to raise significant ethical dilemmas for practitioners, and resistance from those concerned with the erosion of civil liberties.

Whilst Box B and Box C errors can be reduced, it is usually at the expense of increasing the other type of error (Moore, 1996), and not by increasing true positive or true negative predictions. Tolerance of false positives and false negatives can be a matter of moral and political acceptability. Within child abuse prediction for example, tolerance of false negative predictions (that is, no harm will come to a child) can be low (e.g. the Beckford Enquiry, London Borough of Brent, 1985). However, this does not prevent public outcry in cases of false positive prediction and over-intervention (e.g. Cleveland, Butler-Schloss 1988).

Actuarial versus clinical methods

There are two basic approaches to risk assessment and prediction for offenders:

- the *actuarial*; and,

- the *clinical*.

The following section provides a summary of each approach.

Actuarial assessment

Actuarial risk assessment is based upon statistical calculations of probability. Well used in the insurance industry (Green, 1997), actuarial methods for offender risk prediction utilise the basic methodology pioneered by Burgess (1936) for parole violation. From the study of a large number of cases, certain factors that statistically relate to risk, are selected. These are then retrospectively validated by application to cases with a low expectancy of risk and to those with a high expectancy of risk. Risk factors are then retrospectively validated in terms of statistical probabilities. Such factors are often referred to as *static* risk factors as they are deemed largely unchangeable and rooted in historical and demographic factors. Whilst the method has greater accuracy than clinical assessment (Milner and Campbell, 1985; Quinsey et al, 1998), the approach does have its difficulties. These fall under three main headings:

- statistical fallacy;

- limitations within meta-analysis; and,

- low base rates.

(a) Statistical fallacy

Heyman (1997) has argued that probabilities can reduce the uncertainty of risk by '...attributing aggregate properties of a category to individuals within that category...'. A central principle of the actuarial method is a comparison of the similarities of an individual's profile to the aggregated knowledge of past events. The extent to which information from a population can be generalised and applied accurately to the individual under assessment is, however, problematic. This is more commonly known as the 'statistical fallacy' (Dingwall, 1989).

For instance, in reviewing a number of prediction studies, Grubin and Wingate (1996: 353) identified that empirical evidence from one population does not necessarily translate to another, and that most prediction scores cluster at around the 40% mark. They commented that even if this figure represented 'a significant improvement over chance, [it] is not particularly helpful to those who must make decisions about release'. Such predictions merely state that 40 cases in 100 are a potential risk; the method cannot identify with absolute reliability the likely risk in any individual case. They observed that in Quinsey et al's study (1995a) only 3% of the sample (that is, just six men) had 'clinically meaningful' scores of around 85% (i.e. a risk score indicating an 85% probability of future risky behaviour). This highlights the problem of transferring actuarial data about groups to prediction about individuals. In addition, classification profiles can alter as what is known changes over time (hence, insurance companies revise their premiums over time).

(b) Limitations of meta-analysis

The predictive accuracy of actuarial techniques is further tested when meta-analysis is the preferred methodology for establishing actuarial predictors. Meta-analysis is a statistically-based technique that analyses the outcomes of a large volume of primary research studies. These outcomes are then aggregated in order to establish which factors and outcomes have the most statistical significance for risk prediction (McGuire, 1997). In risk, meta-analysis has been used to establish those factors which have the most predictive utility.

However, a number of difficulties exist with this approach. As Grubin and Wingate (1996: 356) state, 'meta-analysis is not particularly good at demonstrating multi-variant effects, which require methodologies of a more complex type...'. In other words, they are not good at identifying a range of possible effects and their interaction. In offender risk prediction more specifically, meta-analysis also has its limitations. Copas (1995: 12) has suggested that whilst useful as a 'descriptive mode', its use in drawing inferences from the data as a whole is limited. Complex outcome measures are often simplistically categorised for ease of comparative analysis (Copas, 1995; Mair, 1997), and the selection of the original studies and the statistical methods employed are open to subjective bias (Losel, 1995; McIvor, 1997).

Actuarial risk variables can also have limited clinical use in the field as they rarely *explain* behaviour (Grubin and Wingate, 1996). In essence, this is the distinction between merely predicting that a risk is likely, and explaining and understanding risky behaviours (Pollock et al, 1989). The latter is essential for practitioners responsible for establishing treatment plans and implementing risk management interventions. This is supported by Weist (1981) who has suggested that a detailed analysis of the interaction between personality and situational factors is essential to establishing treatability and in aiding the worker to select the most suitable treatment programme. Such analysis focuses the worker's attention on those situational and clinical factors that can be changed or prevented by targeted interventions.

(c) Low base rates

Low base rates can also present difficulties for accuracy in actuarial risk assessment. The base rate is the known frequency of a behaviour occurring within the population as a whole. It provides the basis for an actuarial prediction of behaviour in similar cases. For behaviours with low base rates, such as child abuse or sexual offending, predictions made without reference to the relevant base rate can lead to error[11]. This is because they are based upon data on infrequently occurring behaviours within small groups of the population.

More recent statistical developments in actuarial research have been able to compensate for this effect through the application of a technique know as 'Relative Operating Characteristic' or ROC (Mossman, 1994; Rice and Harris, 1995). In short, this technique enables actuarial evaluations of violence prediction free from base rate limitations and clinical 'biases for or against Type I or Type II prediction errors'[12] (Mossman, 1994:783). In a re-evaluation of 58 data sets from 44 published studies using the ROC technique, Mossman demonstrated that mental health practitioners' predictions of violence were substantially more accurate than chance, that short term predictions were no more accurate than long-term ones, and that past behaviour was the best predictor of future behaviour (p.783).

In spite of the criticisms of actuarial assessment, it can, however, be used to:

- establish those risk predictors which have a proven track record;

- establish the relevant base rates for clinical assessment;

- increase the accuracy of risk assessments; and,

- increase levels of consistency and reliability.

[11] *In effect, the correlation coefficient is adversely limited by low base rates.*

[12] *Where a Type I prediction error is a false positive prediction, i.e. a prediction of risk that does not happen, and a Type II prediction error is a false negative prediction (a risk is not predicted but does happen).*

Clinical assessment

The clinical method is essentially a diagnostic assessment derived in part from the medical and mental health fields (Monahan, 1981). It is based upon detailed interviewing and observation by the clinician in order to collect information on the social, environmental, behavioural and personality factors that have resulted in harmful behaviour(s) in the past. Howells and Hollin (1989) describe the process as an individualised assessment, usually concerned with providing a diagnosis, establishing treatability, and where release into the community or legal reports are required, predictions of dangerousness (Pollock et al, 1989). However such predictions have been plagued by unreliability (Monahan, 1981; Quinsey et al, 1998).

Imprecise definitions of dangerousness (Brooks, 1984), coupled with a lack of knowledge of relevant base rate behaviours (Gottfredson and Gottfredson, 1993) and flaws in 'subjective inference', have contributed to the limitations in clinical assessment (Kahneman and Tversky, 1973). In particular, clinicians have a limited ability to judge accurately probability, with judgement biased towards the frequency (rather than the probability) of individual events (Kahneman and Tversky, 1973). It is argued that the processing of information on both probability and likely impact is affected by a number of cognitive heuristics or 'rules of thumb', such as the 'availability' heuristic in which the risks being assessed are matched to the information most easily available and recalled (Combs and Slovic, 1979). Clinicians have traditionally preferred to give weight to case-based rather than statistical information (Carroll, 1977; Nisbett et al, 1976; Shah 1978). False risk predictions can also arise from so-called 'creeping determinism' (Fischoff, 1975), which suggests a causal connection between factors in a case where none in fact exists. In order to produce a coherent narrative, it has been argued that causal connections can be literally imputed through clinical assessment (Einhorn, 1986; Pollock et al, 1989).

Pollock et al (1989) contend that three decades of 'vigorous research' has yet to produce the 'scientific knowledge needed to predict violent behaviour' (p.96). However, more recent commentators (Limandri and Sheridan, 1995) have argued that if combined with the appropriate actuarial data, clinically-based interviewing can have an important role in establishing the significant personality and situational factors which can trigger or exacerbate risky behaviour (Megargee, 1976; Prins, 1988). This assists with explanations of behaviour and the planning of treatment interventions, and is seen by some as a more preferable role for clinical assessment (Pollock et al, 1989; Weist 1981). As public protection panels are tasked with detailed assessments of offender behaviours and circumstances, and the formation and implementation of effective risk management strategies, this use of clinical assessment is likely to be more helpful than prediction *per se.*

[13] OASys stands for the Offender Assessment System and is a prison-probation assessment tool for the risk of recidivism which uses both reconviction predictors and criminogenic needs, combined with a risk of harm assessment. OASys is currently the subject of a pilot evaluation.

Structured clinical interviewing around empirically grounded risk factors or 'criminogenic needs' is already in use in the general assessment of recidivism in probation work (for example the Level of Service Inventory-Revised, LSI-R, [Andrews and Bonta, 1995]), and have been incorporated into the piloted national prison-probation risk tool, OASys[13]. Structured clinical assessment has also been used in cognitive self-change programmes for violent offenders (Bush, 1995) and in offending behaviour programmes rooted in the 'What Works' research of Andrews (1995), McGuire and Priestley (1985; 1995), and Ross and Fabiano (1985). In violence assessment, the 1990s saw the development of detailed lists and 'aides memoire' to guide the assessment of clinicians. For example, Webster et al's (1994) ASSESS-LIST was offered as a 'guide' to 'comprehensive inquiry' rather than as a thoroughly evaluated predictive tool (p.46). This was subsequently superseded by the HCR-20 version 2, although this again is described as an 'aide memoire' (Webster et al, 1997:5).

Clinical assessment of sex offenders against children, particularly in terms of their suitability for cognitive-behavioural group treatment programmes, has been assisted in the 1980s and 1990s by theoretical and empirical work in several areas. These include work on:

- predisposing preconditions (Finkelhor, 1984);

- the 'cycle of assault', which emphasises the physiological, psychological, behavioural and situational factors that contribute to sexual offending (Ryan et al, 1987; Wolf, 1984); and,

- the role of 'cognitive distortions' and denial in sex offending (Salter, 1988).

These have resulted in specific models and interviewing tools for sex offender assessment, particularly within probation and prison service assessments (McEwan and Sullivan, 1996). Public protection panels will already have access to such assessments, particularly for those sex offenders subject to parole licence or statutory community supervision by the probation service. However, panels should regard such assessments as *guides* to treatment and risk management plans, and not necessarily as predictions of future levels of risk.

Use of dynamic risk factors

Dynamic risk factors have been described broadly as those factors which change over time, or which can be made to change through treatment and intervention (Quinsey et al, 1998). In the assessment of general offender recidivism, such factors have been labelled as 'criminogenic needs' (e.g. within the LSI-R and OASys).

Whilst it is generally agreed that they do not out-perform static actuarial predictors[14], the role of dynamic factors in establishing treatment and intervention plans is now well established (HMIP, 1998a; Raynor, 1997). As Quinsey et al (1998) point out, their assessment is often more complex due to their variable nature. For example, some may relate to an offender's environment while others may relate to social networks. Some may change naturally with the passage of time, for example levels of maturity, others may need specific interventions such as housing and employment. Others, such as treatment impact may be difficult to assess as discrete from other variables in the offender's life, such as gaining a stable life-style.

Whilst dynamic variables are important, how they should be weighted within risk assessments can present significant problems (Raynor, 1997). Notwithstanding the problems of measuring re-offending rather than re-conviction, dynamic variables are more difficult to measure than criminal history as they are often compiled from differing sources (including the self-report of the offender), and are open to interpretation by the assessor. May's study of over 7,000 offenders concluded, however, that whilst criminal history is the best predictor of re-offending, those offenders with multiple problems are more 'at risk' (May, 1999). Dynamic factors such as drug misuse, accommodation and employment were found to have a 'clear link' to reconviction (p.26), while knowledge of social factors was particularly helpful in predicting reconviction for those cases with little criminal history (p.38). May's study does acknowledge the varying interpretations of social factors by assessors and variations in their recording, and that some so-called 'social factors', such as ethnicity and whether or not the victim of abuse, are not dynamic. May concludes, however, that the identification of relevant social factors 'could help to confirm the notions of the factors that need to be tackled to reduce re-offending' (p.49).

(a) Dynamic factors in violent offending assessment

The particular contribution of dynamic factors to the assessment of *violent* offending have been explored. Hagell (1998) notes that whilst there is 'an emerging consensus that multiple indicators are likely to be more successful than individual factors' (p.56), which dynamic factors apply in each individual case and how factors overlap is still problematic. For some factors, such as substance abuse and the use and availability of weapons, research evidence is either 'unclear or insufficient' (p.57). Personal factors, such as the offender's general disposition or temperament, and cognitive factors, have also been shown as features of dangerousness assessments (Blackburn, 1994; Howells, 1987). Bush (1995) for example identified cognitive distortions as significant features of decisions to offend violently, with 'anti-social logic' used to justify violent behaviour towards others. His Cognitive Self-Change

[14] Note however that Genderau et al (1996) claimed they could predict general recidivism using dynamic variables as well static indicators.

Programme is based upon challenging such anti-social thinking patterns (Bush, 1995). In a West Midlands study of Section 18 and Section 20 offences, Genders and Morrison (1996) found that offenders tended to blame others and justify their actions as 'out of control'. Other personal and temperamental factors such as lack of self-control, lack of victim empathy and high levels of hostility and aggression have been raised as dynamic indicators of violent behaviour (Hare, 1993; Blackburn, 1994; Menzies et al, 1994). However, whilst important in indicating areas for potential intervention, none of these factors can out-predict past history and convictions.

In their study of partner abuse and familial violence Limandri and Sheridan (1995) noted that violence assessment is enhanced by the addition of key dynamic factors such as 'disinhibiting agents', use and availability of weapons, and access and proximity to victims. Whilst their work is limited to partner abuse, critically they suggest that violence prediction is likely to benefit from research into multiple paths to offending.

(b) Dynamic factors in sex offending assessment

In sex offending assessment, cognitive distortions, the cycle of offending (Wolf, 1984) and grooming patterns have gained significance, particularly in probation and prison officer assessments for group work programmes (Abel et al, 1987; McEwan and Sullivan, 1996). Integrated or multi-factoral theories have also been proposed by research in this field (Finkelhor, 1984; Marshall and Barbaree, 1990; Prentky, 1995; Wolf, 1984). These theories stress the importance of personality factors such as: egocentricity, poor self-image, defensiveness, distorted thinking, obsessive thoughts and behaviours, social alienation, and sexual pre-occupation (Scottish Office, 1997).

Prentky (1995) has outlined a number of dynamic factors significant to sex offending (although all will not necessarily be present in each individual case):

- impaired relationships with adults;

- lack of victim empathy;

- extent and nature of anger, particularly whether instrumental or expressive;

- cognitive distortions and rationalisations for offending;

- sexual fantasy and deviant sexual arousal;

- anti-social personality; and,

- impulsivity.

(Prentky, 1995: 159-167).

However, as with dynamic factors for violent offending, dynamic factors in sexual offending can vary between offender types (for example sexual offending against children and offending against adults). Furthermore, the identification and relevance of each variable in individual cases is somewhat dependent upon the judgement of assessors (for example probation officers). As with dynamic factors for general offending and violent offending, dynamic variables in sexual offending have tended to have most significance in the design and delivery of interventions (Proctor, 1996).

Defensible decisions

Carson (1996) notes that risk assessment is a highly fallible undertaking, and that it is unlikely that any method can be found which will provide certainty and 100% levels of accuracy for worker, agency and public. He argues that in a situation where accuracy cannot be guaranteed, the key to decisions withstanding subsequent accountability and public scrutiny is their *'defensibility'*. In other words, how decisions are evaluated with hindsight after negative outcomes have occurred, and whether decisions can be considered to be 'reasonable'. As Carson (1996: 4) notes, whether a 'responsible body of co-professionals would have made the same decision'. This is particularly pertinent for those agencies who carry out risk assessments in the public eye, and where risk assessment failures can be very costly to organisational credibility.

Monahan (1993) has suggested several elements that need to be present for a decision to be defensible, and these can be translated into minimum standards for risk assessment. A defensible decision is therefore made when:

- all reasonable steps have been taken;

- reliable assessment methods have been used;

- information is collected and thoroughly evaluated;

- decisions are recorded;

- staff work within agency policies and procedures; and,

● staff communicate with others and seek information they do not have.

(Kemsḫall, 1996a; 1996b; 1998a; 1998b).

Combined risk assessments

It is now generally accepted that the accuracy and consistency of risk assessments is enhanced by assessment tools which combine actuarial calculations of probability with detailed clinical interviewing to establish the conditions and circumstances under which risky behaviour(s) might occur (Milner and Campbell, 1995; Quinsey et al, 1998). Such tools combine the use of well-established static risk factors such as previous history of behaviours and convictions, with growing clinical and research knowledge on a wide range of dynamic factors. Dynamic factors are increasingly assessed through the use of 'aides memoire' or structured interviewing tools which emphasise those risk factors most proven by research (Raynor, 1997; Webster et al, 1997). Whilst the accuracy of pure actuarial methods is not always outperformed by the addition of clinically assessed dynamic factors (Ditchfield, 1997; Raynor, 1997), combined methods have an important 'value-added' component by identifying behavioural traits, environmental stressors, personal characteristics and social variables which can trigger offending or exacerbate risk. Multi-variate analysis of the risk of reconviction in general offending, and in sexual and violent offending, is now widely accepted as the most useful approach to risk assessment, providing both predictive utility and useful information for the design of treatment programmes and case interventions. The decision-making of public protection panels is likely to benefit not only from the increased accuracy and case specificity that combined methods of risk assessment can provide, but also from the contribution that such an approach can make to treatment selection, case interventions, risk management strategies, and defensible decisions (Monahan, 1993).

Summary

Clinical and actuarial assessment methods each have advantages and disadvantages. Clinical methods have lower levels of accuracy and are open to the subjective bias of the assessor but have much to contribute in understanding behaviours, environmental stressors, and in establishing feasible treatment and management plans. Actuarial methods have greater predictive accuracy, but can be flawed by the 'statistical fallacy' and low incidence of risky behaviours in the population as a whole. Combining both actuarial and clinical approaches is increasingly advocated as the means to improving the quality of decision-making in risk assessment, and supporting reasonable and defensible decisions (Limandri and Sheridan, 1995; Monahan, 1993).

4. Choice of risk assessment tools

Reliable methods of assessing risk are critical in an area where the consequences may affect public protection and the reduction of harm to potential victims, and where practitioners and agencies may be exposed to public accountability, legal liability and media scrutiny (Carson, 1996; Monahan, 1993).

This section considers assessment tools in respect of two types of offenders: sex offenders; and those others who present a potential or actual danger to others through violent offending. It is important to note that risk assessment tools are subject to development and adaptation in what is a rapidly changing area, and new risk tools for violent and sexual offenders are likely to be introduced. Consequently, this review can only reflect the major assessment tools available at time of writing.

Sex offenders

Grubin's review of sex offending against children (1998: 30) confirmed that the most commonly accepted broad factors for the prediction of sex offence recidivism are: 'offending history, deviant sexual arousal patterns, and previous prison sentences'. Hanson and Bussiere's meta-analysis (1998) confirmed static and historical factors such as offending history and choice of stranger victims as predictive of sex offence recidivism.

Grubin (1998) also noted that various risk assessment tools have been developed to harness this range of risk factors into useful predictive tools, but that only two have been extensively studied in America and Britain:

- the 'Rapid Risk Assessment for Sex Offence Recidivism' (RRASOR) (Hanson, 1997); and,

- the 'Structured Anchored Clinical Judgement' (SACJ)[15] (Thornton and Travers, 1991).

[15] *David Thornton has updated and refined SACJ into MATRIX 2000; see below.*

Before looking at these RRASOR and SACJ in detail, it is useful to review briefly a number of tools which been applied in North America. Both the Sex Offender Risk Appraisal Guide (SORAG) (Quinsey et al, 1998) and the Minnesota Sex Offender Screening Tool-Revised (MnSOST-R) (Epperson et al, 1998) have been developed and pursued in United States and Canada. The SORAG is an adaptation of the Violence Risk Appraisal Guide (VRAG) by Quinsey et al and is principally designed for use with men convicted (or committed to mental hospitals) for offences of rape or child molestation (p.119). It is informed by a desire to distinguish appropriately for prediction purposes between variations in sex offenders and their offence preferences (p.121). Briefly summarised, their findings indicate that criminal history, gender (male), relationship to previous victims, and sexual deviance are 'strongly related to sexual and violent re-offending amongst rapists and child molesters... Offenders who are both psychopathic and sexually deviant are the most likely to recidivate' (p.137). The SORAG comprises a fourteen-item multi-variate assessment guide that includes:

- a psychopathy score;

- criminal history score for both non-violent and violent offending;

- criminal history for sex offending;

- history of sexual offending against children or adults;

- age at index offence;

- never married;

- previous response to conditional release;

- phallometrically measured sexual deviance score;

- alcohol abuse; and,

- DSM criteria III for personality disorder.

(Quinsey et al, 1998: 157).

[16] An actuarial prediction free from base rate limitations and clinical bias against Type I and Type II prediction errors (Mossman, 1994: 783).

[17] In other words, the accuracy of probability for the sample as a whole was 62 per cent.

Whilst initially the SORAG has not out-performed the VRAG, and has a prediction (ROC adjusted[16]) score of 0.62[17] (Rice and Harris, 1997), Quinsey et al claim that when adjusted to include more low risk offenders, a ROC score of around 0.70 will be obtained. This they claim, coupled with the grounding of the SORAG in Hanson and Bussiere's meta-analysis (1998), will increase the predictive accuracy of the SORAG. It is currently the subject of further evaluation.

The MnSOST-R was similarly developed to assess rapists and non-familial child molesters. As with the SORAG, a multi-variate approach is used. Sixteen items, also based on those predictors most validated by meta-analysis, are generated covering sexual and non-sexual offence history, victim's age and relationship to the offender, age of offender, treatment history and previous responses, substance abuse, and unstable employment history (Epperson et al, 1998). As with the SORAG, predictive accuracy is claimed by the designers (a score of 0.45), however Hanson and Thornton (2000) interpret this cautiously (p.131), and draw attention to Epperson et al's own acknowledgement that it has yet to be fully cross-validated. Hanlon et al (1999) conducted a retrospective rating of 26 sex offenders between 1993-1994 using the MnSOST and concluded that 'although group mean score for sexual offenders was almost fourteen points higher than that for the non-sexual offenders, groups were very small and differences not statistically significant' (p.76). In addition, Epperson et al (1995) do not recommend its use with intra-familial child molesters as the baseline recidivist rates are low and consequently false-positive rates are high.

This section now concentrates on the RRASOR and SACJ, due to their more extensive evaluation (Hanson and Thornton, 2000), and their likely relevance to police sex offender assessments and the work of multi-agency public protection panels. The section will also review the recent comparison of these two methods, and their combination to form a new tool, STATIC 99 (Hanson and Thornton, 2000), and the transition to MATRIX 2000.

Rapid Risk Assessment for Sex Offence Recidivism (RRASOR)

This is essentially an actuarially-based tool that weights a number of key variables in terms of their predictive utility. The initial seven items were based upon Hanson and Bussiere's meta-analysis (1998), and subsequently four were substantiated as having predictive accuracy for sex offence recidivism:

- the number of past sex offence convictions or charges (with additional weight given to sex offence history);

- age of the offender is less than 25;

- offender is unrelated to victim; and,

- gender of victim

(Hanson, 1997).

These variables can be scored to produce an overall risk weighting. The ability of the tool to distinguish between high and low risk has been validated with a distinction between an 80% 'low' and 'middle' risk group and a 20% 'high' risk group (Hanson, 1997; Grubin, 1998). It has been extensively tested both on the 'developmental and validation samples' achieving a ROC adjusted score of 0.71 (Hanson and Thornton, 2000).

The Structured Anchored Clinical Judgement (SACJ)

Whilst this tool is clearly rooted in empirical research on sex offence recidivism, it seeks to avoid over-dependence upon static predictors (e.g. age, gender) and archival data (e.g. previous convictions). The tool has a somewhat more dynamic component to allow for changes in risk status over time, and operates as a three-stage 'step-wise' system rather than the 'simple summation of weighted items' (Hanson and Thornton, 2000:121). These comprise:

- Stage 1: initial actuarially-based screening;

- Stage 2: a more in-depth analysis of aggravating factors;

- Stage 3: careful monitoring of offender performance over time to note the impact of treatment on risky dispositions.

The first stage is designed as an initial screening of low, medium and high risk, based upon five items:

- a current sex offence;

- a past conviction(s) for a sexual offence;

- past convictions for non-sexual violence;

- current non-sexual violent offences; and

- four or more previous convictions of any sort.

(Hanson and Thornton, 2000:121).

Four or more factors mean high risk, two to three mean medium risk, and less than two means low risk. Stage 2 adds key dymanic factors (Hanson and Thornton, 2000:121):

- any stranger victims;

- any male victims;

- never married;

- convictions for non-contact sex offences (e.g. obscene phone calls);

- substance abuse;

- placement in residential care as a child;

- deviant sexual arousal; and,

- psychopathy, a score of 25+ on the PCL-R (see below).

If two or more of these factors are present then the risk category is increased by one category.

Stage 3 considers in-depth clinical information on treatment response and progress, and any improvement in relation to dynamic risk factors. This stage was particularly developed to monitor progress on prison treatment programmes and has been less well evaluated than Stages 1 and 2. In addition, Stages 2 and 3 are heavily dependent upon the availability of clinical data and information on dynamic factors. To compensate for this, a shortened version of the SACJ using Stage 1 and the first four variables of Stage 2 and known as SACJ-MIN can be used (Hanson and Thornton, 2000). The SACJ-MIN has been validated on approximately 500 sex offenders released from HM Prisons in 1979 and subjected to a 16-year follow-up. In this sample, 'the SACJ-MIN correlated 0.34 with sex offence recidivism and 0.30 with any sexual or violent recidivism', although the tool has yet to be extensively tested outside the United Kingdom prison population (Hanson and Thornton, 2000:122).

SACJ-MIN is already in extensive use in police sex offender assessments in registration units, and to a more limited extent in multi-agency public protection assessments (Maguire et al, 2001). The Association of Chief Police Officers (ACPO) working party on sex offender risk assessment has recommended the adoption of the SACJ-MIN as an initial screening tool (ACPO, 1999).

Combining RRASOR and SACJ-MIN: the development of STATIC 99

RRASOR and the SACJ-Min were compared in four diverse samples from the United Kingdom and Canada, and 'showed roughly equivalent predictive accuracy' (Hanson and Thornton, 2000:119). Both scales have since been combined to produce STATIC 99 (Hanson and Thornton, 1999). Data from the four same samples indicate that STATIC 99 outperformed both the RRASOR and SACJ-MIN, although Hanson and Thornton state that the 'incremental improvement of the STATIC 99 was relatively small' (p.129), with a ROC adjusted score of 0.71 for sexual recidivism, and a ROC adjusted score of 0.69 for violent (including sexual) recidivism (p.129). In comparison to other methods, STATIC 99 has a similar predictive accuracy as the SORAG based upon one data set only, but does not outperform the MnSOST-R. The latter has not, however, been subjected to cross-validation.

STATIC 99 is a developing tool, and Hanson and Thornton note that 'actuarial risk scales can improve on STATIC 99 by including dynamic (changeable) risk factors as well as additional static variables' (Hanson and Thornton, 1999 p. 131). Three additional indicators of sexual deviance, repetitive victim choice and early onset of sexual offending, are suggested.

MATRIX 2000

Since the comparison of three actuarial scales by Hanson and Thornton (2000) and the development of STATIC 99 for use in Canada, Thornton has updated and refined SACJ into MATRIX 2000, and this has been rapidly adopted by police forces for sex offender assessment (Risk Assessment and Management of Sex Offenders Police Conference, Cheltenham, October 2000). The tool represents an important improvement on SACJ as it provides for greater accuracy and refinement in the identification of very high-risk offenders, and offers two versions, one for sex offenders and one for violent offenders. Whilst the tool has not yet been subject to extensive published evaluations, it has been validated retrospectively against a twenty-year follow up of reconvictions and identified a very high risk group (comprising 13% of the sample), of whom 60% were reconvicted. This type of categorisation enables more accurate targeting around very high-risk offenders. Similar findings have been found for a sample of violent offenders (Grubin, 2000).

In addition, MATRIX 2000 advocates the combining of actuarial factors such as general criminogenic risk factors and a sexually deviant lifestyle, with dynamic risk factors, such as lifestyle, negative peer influences, psychological factors (e.g. negative attitudes, poor self-management and problem-solving), and acute factors (such as precipitating situational factors, denial, access to victims, and psychological distress) (Grubin, 2000).

Usefulness of sex offender tools to police service risk assessments

The RRASOR, SACJ, and the STATIC 99 all have relevance to the initial screening of sex offenders in police sex offender registration units, and to the work of public protection panels in determining levels of risk. To date the SACJ, particularly SACJ-MIN has been preferred (ACPO, 1999; Maguire et al, 2001) and has been adapted and refined into MATRIX 2000 in order to identify more accurately very high risk offenders. However, all the tools are limited to male offenders, and are designed to predict recidivism and not levels of seriousness or harm; they are therefore unlikely to operate as 'stand alone' instruments in public protection panel work. Their contribution is likely to be in the selection of high risk individual cases for further panel consideration.

Violent offenders

Traditionally, unacceptable levels of unreliability have plagued violence prediction. The research literature on dangerousness and the development of assessment tools for violence prediction derive predominantly from the mental health field and reflect psychiatric concerns to predict dangerousness accurately. Assessment tools have therefore been developed largely for use with mental health in-patients, psychiatric assessments at point of sentence, or prisoners under consideration for parole. Research populations have been largely male and institutionalised, and transferability to other offenders is acknowledged as problematic. As Hagell (1998: 69) states, the tools vary in their 'definitions, purposes and the quality of evaluation' and consequently the reliability of tools both in the field, and in terms of producing accurate predictions, has been questioned (Menzies et al, 1994). Due to their empirical rooting in particular populations, violent behaviours and victim groups, assessment tools tend to be highly specific, and this remains a barrier to the development of a single all-embracing tool. Against this background, comparative evaluations are limited, as like cannot necessarily be compared with like. This section will examine those assessment tools most discussed in the research literature in the United States, Canada and the UK, and focus on those most likely to have relevance to the assessment of violent offenders coming before multi-agency public protection panels. The assessment tools are discussed under three main headings: actuarial tools; structured clinical tools; and multi-factoral tools.

Actuarial violence assessment

The **Violence Risk Assessment Guide** (VRAG) (Quinsey et al, 1998) is the most widely used actuarial tool for violence offence recidivism (Cooke, 2000). The VRAG was developed in Canada, based upon patients detained in secure hospitals between 1965 and 1980, and has been the subject of extensive evaluation (Quinsey et al, 1998). The VRAG contains twelve items:

- Revised Psychopathy Checklist score

- Elementary School Maladjustment score

- Meets DSM III criteria for any personality disorder

- Age at time of index offence

- Separation from either parent (except death) under age 16

- Failure on prior conditional release

- Non-violent offence history score (using the Cormier-Lang scale)

- Never married

- Meets DSM III criteria for schizophrenia

- Most serious victim injury (from the index offence)

- Alcohol abuse score

- Female victim in the index offence

(Quinsey et al, 1998:147).

The factors are scored using a weighting system 'that calculates the weight on the basis of how different the individual is from the base rate' (p.147). Based upon a number of evaluations (Harris et al, 1993; Rice and Harris, 1995; Quinsey et al, 1995) the VRAG has an adjusted ROC score between 0.73 and 0.77. The VRAG score is used to assign individuals to one of nine risk categories (or 'bins' as Quinsey et al designate them) and an individual's 'actual risk scores' does not differ 'by more than one "bin" from his obtained score' (p.150). The VRAG is subject to on-going evaluation (Quinsey, et al 1998) but has established a reputation for predictive accuracy (Cooke, 2000).

The VRAG does, however, have recognised limits. First, the probability prediction of recidivism does not include any assessment or prediction of the nature, severity, imminence, and frequency of future violence (Cooke, 2000). Secondly, statements on the probability of recidivism over long periods of time (for example five, seven or ten years) do not assist individual case managers or panels in planning risk management strategies in specific cases where issues of severity and imminence can be more important. Finally, the VRAG encourages assessors to ignore clinical and dynamic factors outside the 12 items even in the face of research which may show their relevance to violent behaviour (Cooke, 2000; Hart, 1999). It is difficult to see that such decisions would be defensible in the light of risk assessment failures.

The **Violence Prediction Scheme** (VPS) of Webster et al, (1994) is designed for the assessment of dangerousness in high risk men. The scheme utilises the twelve items of the VRAG (called RAG) to produce an actuarial score, combined with structured assessment of ten, largely dynamic, items[18]. The authors acknowledge that the addition of the dynamic ASSESS-LIST adds very little to the accuracy of the actuarial (V)RAG score, however they stress the importance of the structured clinical assessment for the establishment of treatability and formulation of appropriate risk management plans (Webster et al, 1994:57). The further development of structured assessment around the **HCR-20** is discussed below.

[18] *Antecedent history, self presentation, social and psychological adjustment, expectations and plans, symptoms, supervision, life factors, institutional management, sexual adjustment, and treatment progress (Webster et al, 1994:47)*

Structured assessment tools

The **HCR-20** is a systematic model for assessing the risk of violence. The assessment combines historical factors that have a track record in predicting risk, with clinical variables such as respondent insight, attitude, motivation to change and to treatment, stability, and general symptomology. In addition, the assessment tool has the 'value-added' component of structuring the assessor's attention towards case management plans, motivation to change and individual coping mechanisms. The HCR-20 is divided into three sub-scales:

Historical Scale

● Previous violence

● Young age at first violent incident

● Relationship instability

● Employment problems

● Substance use problems

● Major mental illness

● Psychopathy

● Early maladjustment

● Personality disorder

● Prior supervision failure

Clinical Scale

- Lack of insight

- Negative attitudes

- Active symptoms of major mental illness

- Impulsivity

- Unresponsive to treatment

Risk Management Scale

- Plans lack feasibility

- Exposure to destabilisers

- Lack of personal support

- Non-compliance with remediation attempts

- Stress

(Webster et al, 1997: 11)

Whilst initially formulated as an 'aide memoire' in order to make decisions transparent (Webster et al, 1997: pp.5, 73), the predictive validity of the HCR-20 has been evaluated (Douglas et al, 1999) with persons 'scoring above the HCR-20 median… six to thirteen times more likely to be violent than those scoring below the median' (p.917). In this evaluative study, the HCR-20 was found to add incremental validity to the Psychopathy Checklist-Screening Version (PCL-SV), although the sample was restricted to civil psychiatric patients.

This research validated the importance of the *Historical* and *Risk Management* scales (with the *Clinical* scale having a limited significance to short-term risk prediction), and the dynamic factors were seen as particularly pertinent to the ongoing assessment of risk. Cooke's short review of the HCR-20 (2000) indicates that these findings have been supported by Klassen's evaluation of the Historical Scale of the HCR-20. This found a 'moderate strength correlation' to in-patient violence by civil psychiatric patients (Klassen, 1999). Further work by Strand et al (1999) revealed that the HCR-20 was related to violence, while Wintrup's study (1996) found a moderate strength correlation to patients who committed violence after release from secure forensic settings. However, limits to this study were acknowledged. The small scale of the sample (193 patients) over a relatively short time frame (626 days) does require longer follow-up, particularly post-discharge.

In a prospective study of 41 long-term sentenced offenders in two high-security prisons, Belfrage et al (2000) found that the *Historical* scale was of little use for high risk men, but that there was a high predictive value for the *Clinical* and *Risk Management* scales. These two scales can provide more sensitive discrimination for high risk groups (p.173). The tool has however been almost exclusively applied in the mental health arena. Furthermore, as with other methods, severity and impact of offending are less well covered (Douglas et al, 1999).

Whilst not the subject of a direct comparison, the above evaluation of the HCR-20 suggests that it will out-perform the **Dangerous Behaviour Rating Scheme** (DBRS) (Menzies et al, 1994). The DBRS includes a variety of items such as personality attributes, situational variables, triggers for violence, and inhibitors of violence. It was developed for the assessment of dangerousness for pre-trial forensic patients.

The DBRS is a semi-structured tool and has been subject to a rigorous six-year follow-up. The outcome was not positive with Menzies et al concluding that 'a standardized, reliable, generalizable set of criteria for dangerousness prediction…. is still an elusive and distant objective' (Menzies et al, 1994: 25).

Psychopathy and violence prediction

The identification of psychopathy and links to violence prediction has also preoccupied researchers (for instance, Hare, 1991; Hare and Hart, 1993). Hart et al, (1994) define psychopathy as a distinct personality disorder comprising interpersonal, affective and behavioural symptoms. These are expressed in terms of egocentricity, emotional coldness and manipulation of others, lack of empathy and remorse, and a tendency towards anti-social behaviour and violation of social norms. In relation to these offenders, Hare's psychopathy checklist has gained increasing currency in forensic settings as a structured interviewing tool. It has also been found effective in predicting those offenders most likely to violate parole (Hart et al, 1994), and those young male offenders most likely to re-offend (Forth et al, 1990).

The **Psychopathy Check List-Revised** (PCL-R) and its derivatives (the PCL:YV for adolescents and the PCL:SV 'screening version'[19]) is a clinical construct rating scale used in semi-structured interview. A total of 20 items are rated on a three-point scale and divided into three broad categories:

[19] *The 'Hare P Scan' is being developed for work with Probation in Canada. Hare, R. D. and Herve, H. (1999) The Hare P-Scan. Toronto: Multi-Health Systems.*

Interpersonal/affective:

- Glibness/superficial charm

- Grandiose sense of self-worth

- Pathological lying

- Conning/manipulative

- Lack of remorse or guilt

- Shallow affect

- Failure to accept responsibility

Social deviance:

- Need for stimulation/proneness to boredom

- Parasitic lifestyle

- Poor behavioural controls

- Early behavioural problems

- Lack of realistic long-term goals

- Impulsivity

- Irresponsibility

- Juvenile delinquency

Additional items:

- Promiscuous sexual behaviour

- Many short-term marital relationships

- Criminal versatility

(Hare, 1991: 1, 73-77).

Whilst initially developed from research on male forensic patients and offenders, various studies have confirmed the applicability of the PCL-R to other offender and patient populations. These include women, ethnic minorities and offenders from different cultures (Brown and Forth, 1997; Cooke, 1998; Cooke et al, 1998; Hare, 1998). Various studies have established that the PCL-R can identify psychopathy accurately amongst forensic patients (Cooke and Mitchie, 1999; Hare, 1991; McDermott et al, 2000) with interpersonal and affective items proving to be more discriminating (Cooke et al, 1998). It is highly reliable when used by well-trained assessors. Meta-analysis by Salekin et al (1996) has established PCL-R as a robust risk predictor for violence recidivism, with psychopathic prisoners four times more likely to offend violently within one year of release. Harris et al (1993) found that the PCL-R was the best predictor of future violence for those released from a maximum security unit and a pre-trial psychiatric assessment centre. Subsequently the PCL-R score was integrated into the VRAG assessment criteria. Hare (2000) has stated that whilst the PCL was not designed as a measurement of violence risk, it may measure the most important factor in the risk of predatory violence (i.e. psychopathy).

The PCL-R is currently the subject of an evaluation on male offenders from the Prison Service in England. The PCL screening version, designed for use as a stand alone screening tool for use with forensic patients including non-criminal civil patients, is currently the subject of evaluation under the MacArthur Risk Assessment study (Steadman et al, 1999). The latter forms one example of a multi-factoral approach discussed below.

Multi-factoral approaches and classification trees

The **MacArthur** assessment tool is part of a long term study into the release of patients from acute psychiatric hospitals into the community and is used for the assessment of mentally disordered offenders. It is extensively reviewed in Steadman et al, (1994), and it is of interest due to the emphasis placed upon a multi-factoral approach to violence prediction. The tool allocates risk factors to four general categories:

- *dispositional factors* (demographic factors such as age, gender, social class, as well as particular personality variables);

- *historical factors* (factors that highlight the patient's life history including family and employment history, as well as a history of violent behaviour by the patient);

- *contextual factors* (social supports and relevant social networks, access to victims and weapons); and,

- *clinical factors* (distinct mental or personality disorders, and factors which affect stability and personal functioning such as drug and alcohol abuse).

(Steadman et al, 1994: 302-303).

The tool is open to criticism because the boundaries between categories may not always be clear. For example, some 'demographic' factors could be re-framed as 'clinical' ones. Furthermore, the relative weighting of the different factors in terms of their role as predisposing factors in risk is not made clear.

The tool does, however, usefully distinguish between those risk factors which are dynamic and hence most amenable to change and intervention (e.g. 'contextual' and 'clinical' factors), and those which are static and unlikely to diminish (those which are 'demographic' and 'historical'). This can helpfully guide practitioners' interventions towards those factors most likely to change.

Classification trees are another recent example of a multi-factoral approach (Monahan et al, 2000; Steadman et al, 1999). In essence, the **Iterative Classification Tree** (ICT) takes a binary approach to risk decision making. Assessors follow a pre-set guide through a series of options, applying questions that are empirically and theoretically grounded, with each question dependent upon the answer to the preceding one. The model starts with initial screening (for example using the PCL-R) and the classification is refined through the questioning process. The ICT is designed to assist practitioners with the efficient use of actuarial data in clinical settings (Monahan et al, 2000:312). The ICT 'partitioned 72.6% of a sample of discharged psychiatric patients into one of two categories with regard to their risk of violence to others during the first 20 weeks after discharge' (p. 317). However, as Monahan et al (2000) point out, this approach can only classify individuals as either high or low risk (p.312). A number of individuals remain unclassified. As Cooke (2000) states, 'it is these individuals, whose risk level is equivocal, with whom the assessor needs most assistance' (p.154).

Relevance and selection of assessment instruments

As note above, neither sex offenders nor violent offenders can be considered as homogeneous groups (Grubin, 1998; Walker, 1996). The range of offending, settings, and victims is diverse. This makes transferability of assessment instruments across offender groups difficult, and can also raise issues of specificity in the application of a single tool to whole categories of offenders. The field of risk assessment is also subject to continuing development and it is likely that in due course other tools will be introduced. Of those reviewed for violent offending:

- the VRAG is the most robust predictor of future violence *per se*;

- the HCR-20 provides both prediction, and identification of areas pertinent to the formulation of treatment interventions and risk management strategies, particularly for forensic and prison populations;

- the PCL-R has a proven track record for the identification of psychopathy and for the prediction of predatory violence across a number of offender types (including women and ethnic minorities); and,

- the multi-factoral approaches and classification trees are largely restricted to the forensic field and are the subject of on-going evaluation. However, their inability to classify adequately medium risk offenders is problematic (Cooke, 2000).

It is unlikely that multi-agency public protection panels will directly apply these assessment tools. Panels are more likely to experience them as the assessments provided by expert personnel (such as psychiatrists) or from other agencies, for example:

- upon the release of individuals from prison or psychiatric care;

- or as part of probation service assessments for community-based treatment programmes; and,

- in the case of the SACJ, from police sex offender registration units.

Multi-agency panels will, however, have to base their risk assessment decisions and risk management strategies upon information generated by these tools, and personnel should therefore have a basic understanding of their purpose and how they are used.

Summary

The risk assessment of sex offenders is now informed by two main tools, the RRASOR and the SACJ. The latter has been most extensively used in England, particularly in the prison service and in police service sex offender registration units. STATIC 99 offers value-added predictive accuracy to both the RRASOR and SACJ, without compromising the dynamic aspect of the SACJ tool. More recently, SACJ has been updated and refined into MATRIX 2000, and this has been quickly adopted for sex offender risk assessment in the UK.

Numerous tools inform the risk assessment of violent offenders, with the VRAG in most common use and with the widest application. The PCL-R has a more restricted role, but has been usefully integrated into other assessment tools, such as the VRAG. The HCR-20 offers additional clinical and risk management information to case managers tasked with treatment or case planning.

More recent approaches offer an interesting combination of tools and classification trees, but remain at a largely evaluative stage and do not capture the medium risk classification of key concern to practitioners. It is likely that assessment tools will continue to develop and that further tools will be introduced in due course.

Multi-agency public protection panels are unlikely to directly apply these tools, but will have to use such assessments from other personnel and relevant agencies to inform their decision making on both risk assessment and management.

5. Risk management of sexual and violent offenders

The supervision of high risk persons in the community is one of the most complex and difficult tasks currently facing criminal justice personnel. It is one area where the credibility and effectiveness of criminal justice agencies is harshly measured, particularly in the light of serious incidents and risk management failures. However, the effective risk management of offenders is seen as central to public protection through the prevention or reduction of harmful behaviours (Home Office, 1997b).

While risks cannot necessarily be prevented, they can be reduced (Laws, 1996; Ryan, 1996). Risk management should therefore be understood as risk *reduction* rather than *prevention*, that is, reducing:

- the factors which lead to risks occurring; or

- the impact of the risk once it has occurred.

This approach is more commonly known as 'harm reduction' (Laws, 1996) and is widely used in the treatment of drugs and alcohol abuse. The key principle of harm reduction is that reduction in the frequency of harmful behaviours is a gain, as this reduces the number of victims, and, that any positive change in harmful behaviours will lessen the impact of such behaviours on others.

This section reviews the risk management strategies most likely to assist multi-agency public protection panels in their work, and is therefore selective rather than exhaustive. Specific case management protocols and current examples of best practice are addressed in Maguire et al (2001). The section will cover the following areas:

- Intervention programmes; and

- Intensive risk management strategies of community control, using supervision, monitoring, surveillance, and enforcement.

Intervention programmes

These are defined as programmes designed to assist offenders to change their criminal behaviour through control and/or management of thinking patterns, feelings, drives and attitudes (Scottish Office, 1997: 34). Programmes may use a range of methods, but in practice they have been based upon intensive cognitive-behavioural methods delivered both residentially (for example in custody) and within the community (Vennard and Hedderman, 1998).

Sex offenders

Beckett's survey of cognitive-behavioural programmes for sex offenders found that most programmes focused on four main areas:

● Changing patterns of deviant sexual arousal;

● Correcting distorted thinking and educating offenders in the 'cycle of abuse';

● Educating offenders about the effects and impact of abuse; and,

● Increasing social competence.

(Beckett, 1994).

Proctor's study for the Association of Chief Officers of Probation found that probation programmes also contained the following key elements:

● Victim empathy;

● Controlling sexual arousal;

● Reducing denial; and,

● Improving family relationships.

(Proctor, 1996).

Evaluation of programmes has been hindered by the small numbers involved, variation in programme objectives and content, diverse offender and offence types within programmes, and differences in the severity of offending (Quinsey et al, 1993). Notwithstanding these difficulties, both evaluative studies (Barbaree, 1997; Barker and Morgan, 1993; Marshall and Barbaree, 1988; Marshall et al, 1991; Marshall et al, 1999) and meta-analysis (Hall, 1995; Nagayama-Hall, 1995) have indicated that cognitive-behavioural programmes are the most promising, particularly for non-familial child molesters. Nagayama-Hall's (1995) meta-analysis of twelve studies found that cognitive-behavioural treatments and hormonal treatments were significantly more effective than behavioural treatment alone, although not significantly different from one another. However, cognitive-behavioural treatment enjoyed better compliance rates than hormonal treatments (p.807).

Based on these studies, and more recent evaluations such as Hedderman and Sugg's study for the Home Office (1996), Beckett et al (1994) on seven treatment programmes, and Beech et al's evaluation of the prison Sex Offender Treatment Programme (1999), it is possible to conclude that cognitive-behavioural methods have a growing track-record of effectiveness with sex offenders. The following limited conclusions can be drawn:

- Overall, cognitive-behavioural programmes can have a positive effect on offenders' attitudes and recidivism rates. This is supported by the Home Office longitudinal study limited to child sex offenders (Hedderman and Sugg, 1996; Beckett et al, 1994; Beech et al, 1999).

- Amenability to treatment is important. Certain patterns of sex offending are more difficult to treat than others. For example, serious and well-established behaviours involving penetrative sex and violence (e.g. rape) are less amenable to treatment (Waterhouse et al, 1994). Waterhouse et al, (1994) therefore suggested the following factors are significant in establishing treatability:

  - the nature of the offence;
  - the acceptance of responsibility by the offender;
  - the motivation to change by the offender; and,
  - the type of offender.

(adapted from A Commitment to Protect, Scottish Office, 1997)[20].

[20] This text also provides more detailed information on the goals and elements of sex offender programmes (Scottish Office, 1997).

- Timing of interventions can be crucial. Beckett et al (1994) have argued that intensive challenge during 'denial' can be counter-productive as this reduces the likelihood of establishing victim empathy. They noted that improvement required a significant therapeutic input, and that 25% of the offenders actually deteriorated in terms of victim empathy. They attributed this to the early timing of the intervention before offenders had come to terms with the consequences of their actions. In a climate that challenged their activities, offenders developed a strategy of blaming victims in order to cope with confrontation.

- Programme integrity is also important. In a small-scale assessment of a community-based treatment programme for sex offenders, Allam (1998) found that programmes must be delivered as specified and that skills for offender self-risk management and relapse prevention are often inadequate when an offender leaves the programme. However, the majority of sex offenders did improve with treatment.

The more recent evaluation of the prison Sex Offender Treatment Programme (SOTP) (Beech et al, 1999) supports the view that cognitive-behavioural treatments are particularly effective with child abusers. Four main areas were subject to psychometric testing before and after treatment: denial/admittance of sexual deviance and offending; pro-offending attitudes; predisposing personality factors; and relapse prevention skills (p.6). Analysis of the impact of treatment upon denial and deviancy levels revealed greater effectiveness for low deviancy/low denial men (59% showing an overall treatment effect and 84% showing a significant reduction in pro-offending attitudes). Low deviancy and high denial men were less successful (17% showing an overall treatment effect and 71% showing a significant reduction in pro-offending attitudes). High deviancy and high denial were the least successful group (with 14% showing an overall treatment effect and 43% showing a significant reduction in pro-offending attitudes) (p.7). The study also showed that the longer 160-hour programme was more effective. Whilst some prisoners have since been followed up in the community, it is too early for longer-term evaluation based upon reconviction rates.

Violent offenders

The evaluation of risk management strategies for violent offenders is also restricted by the paucity of outcome studies and by the severe ethical and methodological difficulties in constructing control groups. Studies have mostly occurred within psychiatric residential hospitals (Rice, 1997; Rice et al, 1992; Webster et al, 1995), the case management of mentally-ill persons in the community (Dvoskin and Steadman, 1994), or the evaluation of domestic violence programmes (Dobash et al, 1999). Rice's study of interventions in a mental health hospital has also suggested that some interventions can have unintended consequences, for example the exacerbation of violence amongst psychopaths. Rice contended that this negative outcome was due to treatment raising their self-esteem and thus fuelling their aggression. In addition, psychopaths tended to be 'false compliers', learning to fake empathy and deceive others (Harris et al, 1994). This strongly indicates that risk management interventions must be well matched to the risk of violence presented and the offender group in question.

As with sex offenders, cognitive-behavioural methods have achieved growing success with violent offenders. Generally they have two objectives: to change the violent cognitions of the individual; and to change violent behaviour (Browne and Howells, 1996; Hollin, 1993). Anger management programmes have been developed to address the former (Howells, 1989), and social learning and problem solving programmes to address the latter. Whilst there has been some limited evaluation of the effectiveness of these approaches (Glick and Goldstein, 1987), Browne and

Howells (1996) concluded that whilst 'controlled outcome studies to date are encouraging... few studies have been conducted in which serious violence itself has been the outcome measure' (p.205-206).

More recently the 'cognitive restructuring' and the skills training pioneered by Glick and Goldstein has been incorporated into an intensive Cognitive Self-Change programme for violent men piloted and evaluated in Vermont, Canada (Bush, 1995). The programme targets the:

- distorted cognitions of violent offenders;

- deconstruction of the 'anti-social logic' of offenders, particularly the logic of self-justification (the 'victim stance') for violence and victim blaming;

- reinforcement and reward for violent behaviour;

- promotion of alternative/pro-social thinking patterns; and,

- teaching of problem solving skills.

(Bush, 1995: 142-148).

Follow-up evaluation has tracked offenders from 1988 and has compared the recidivism rates of those who completed the programme and those who did not (in the study recidivism is defined broadly to include any accusation as opposed to conviction). The differences in recidivism rates are statistically significant, with only 45.5% of those who had experienced the programme having a further accusation after three years, compared to 76.6% who had not experienced the programme (p.152-153). In the UK, violent offender programmes based on cognitive-behavioural methods are being used in prisons and probation, and are subject to development and evaluation under the Home Office 'Pathfinder' programme.

An important feature of the programme is its integration into a broader risk management strategy, which emphasises intensive supervision comprising: surveillance, alcohol and drug testing, reincarceration for any violations, and strong enforcement of rules and requirements. These features of risk management are discussed below.

Community risk management: supervision, monitoring, surveillance and enforcement

Critically, the Vermont programme recognises that the promotion of offender internal controls needs to be balanced with the implementation of external controls. Key features of the system are early response to signs of relapse (such as failure to attend appointments) and systematic monitoring of progress including behaviour checks and the use of self-report on activities and thinking patterns. Treatment interventions and control are integrated into a broader risk management strategy, in which the supervisor is responsible for co-ordinating the strategy, ensuring appropriate monitoring and surveillance, and action to enforce conditions and controls as appropriate.

Some offenders are not amenable to treatment, or their motivation to comply with treatments/programmes remains low. In these cases, high levels of community control may be the only risk management option coupled with strict enforcement of any conditions and the appropriate use of sanctions (such as parole recall or returns to court for breach of community penalities) (HMIP, 1998b).

Similar risk management strategies exist for high risk sex offenders, such as the Sexually Violent Predator programme in Phoenix, Arizona (MacLean, 2000). In addition to a therapeutic component, such programmes emphasise:

● strong incentives for individuals to manage their own behaviour;

● strong incentives to attend and comply with therapy/programmes;

● a thorough system of supervision with regular re-assessment;

● clear boundaries for acceptable behaviour and enforcement; and,

● integrated management of custody, therapy and community services.

(from MacLean, 2000:59)

In a review of intensive case management for the reduction of violence by mentally ill persons in the community, Dvoskin and Steadman (1994) make a number of useful points which could also be applied to community case management of high risk offenders. These include:

- the need for regular monitoring to note changes in, and to take action on, individual and situational factors which result in violence or sexual harm;

- offenders should be assisted in gaining insight into high risk situations and to develop techniques for self-risk management;

- case *management* responsibility should be clearly vested in one person;

- there should be continuity of case management, both in terms of personnel and intervention strategies;

- there should be speedy access to support services (e.g. appropriate mental health care); and,

- there should be appropriate power and authority to limit risky behaviours and to enforce requirements which diminish risk (e.g. parole recall, breach of community orders).

In their report, *Exercising constant vigilance: The role of the Probation Service in Protecting the Public from Sex Offenders* (1998), Her Majesty's Inspector of Probation (HMIP) also stress the importance of multi-agency co-operation, constant vigilance, monitoring and enforcement. Multi-agency public protection panels are clearly arenas in which such broader risk management strategies can be developed and their implementation subsequently reviewed.

Summary: risk management of sexual and violent offenders

Evaluation of cognitive-behavioural programmes have yielded some of the best results for the effective treatment of both sexual and violent offenders. Appropriate targeting and matching of offenders to programmes is also emphasised, and the integration of such programmes into broader strategies of risk management is advocated. Strategies that emphasise the promotion of internal controls, with the imposition of clear external ones, are increasingly stressed as the key to the successful risk management of high risk offenders in the community.

Intensive supervision, monitoring, surveillance, and enforcement of rules and sanctions coupled with cognitive behavioural intervention programmes are the key features of effective high risk management strategies.

---

6. Conclusion

The effective and reliable assessment and management of sexual and violent offenders is a pressing issue. Both offence types, but particularly violent sexual crime and paedophilia, are attracting increasing public and media attention. In this climate it is essential that police personnel can fulfil their duties to identify, assess and register sex offenders, and where appropriate, contribute to the effective assessment and management of dangerous offenders. Combined actuarial and clinical methods can contribute to effective risk assessment, and numerous methods exist for both sexual and violent offenders. In selecting any method is it is essential that consideration be given to:

- the transferability of the method to the field;

- the distinction between initial screening and individual assessment and case planning;

- the specificity of the tool to the offender group and behaviour in question; and,

- the reliability and validity of the tool.

(from Webster et al, 1995)

The RRASOR and the SACJ both have utility in initial screening for high risk sex offenders, and the SACJ has greater 'value-added' in terms of the dynamic factors. The newly combined STATIC 99 has out-performed both tools and is subject to on-going evaluation.

Seven assessment tools in respect of violent offenders have been reviewed, covering actuarial, structured assessment tools, and multi-factoral and classification tree approaches. Of these the VRAG is the most accurate and most widely used, although other tools such as the HCR-20 provide added value in terms of identifying dynamic factors for case intervention and treatment.

In terms of risk management, there is increasing information on effective programmes and case management for both sexual and violent offenders. It is suggested that panel personnel are familiar with such programmes and that panels give due consideration to matching offenders to the most effective interventions, in addition to identifying more clearly those who require higher levels of community surveillance. Panels have a key role in the effective implementation of integrated risk management strategies, combining both cognitive-behavioural programmes and intensive community supervision.

References

Abel, G., Becker, K., Mittelman, M., Cunningham-Rather, J. and Murphy, W. (1987) 'Self-reported sex crimes of non-incarcerated paraphiliacs', *Journal of Interpersonal Violence* 2: 3-25.

Allam, J. (1998) *Men who sexually abuse children - an evaluation of treatment effectiveness: 0-50 hours data.* Interim report prepared for West Midlands Probation Service.

Andrews, D. A. (1995) 'The psychology of criminal conduct and effective treatment', in McGuire, J. (ed) *What Works: Reducing Reoffending. Guidelines from research and practice.* Chichester: John Wiley: 35-62.

Andrews, D. A. and Bonta, J. (1995) *The Level of Supervision Inventory-Revised.* Toronto: Multi-Health Systems Inc.

Association of Chief Police Officers (1999) *Sex Offenders: A Risk Assessment Model.* ACPO Working Party.

Barbaree, M. (1997) 'Evaluating Treatment Efficacy with Sexual Offenders: The Insensitivity of Recidivism Studies to Treatment Effects', *Journal of Research and Treatment*, 9 (2) 111-128.

Barker, M. and Morgan, R. (1993) *Sex Offenders: A Framework for the Evaluation of Community-Based Treatment - A report for the Home Office.* London: Home Office.

Bean, P. (1997) 'Paedophiles and the Proposed Register', *Justice of the Peace and Local Government Law*, March 22: 283-284.

Beckett, R. (1994) 'Cognitive-Behavioural Treatment of Sex Offenders', in Morrision, T. Erooga, M. and Beckett, R. (eds.) *Sexual Offending Against Children: assessment and treatment of male abusers.* London: Routledge.

Beckett, R., Beech, A. Fisher, D. and Fordham, A. S. (1994) *Community-Based Treatment for Sex Offenders: An Evaluation of Seven Treatment Programmes.* A report for the Home Office by the STEP team. London: Home Office.

Beech, A., Fisher, D. and Beckett, R. (1999) Step 3: *An Evaluation of the Prison Sex Offender Treatment Programme. A report for the Home Office by the STEP team.* London: Home Office.

Belfrage, H., Fransson, G. and Strand, S. (2000) 'Prediction of violence using the HCR-20: a prospective study in two maximum-securtiy correctional institutions', *Journal of Forensic Psychiatry*, 11 (1) 167-175.

Blackburn, R. (1994) *The Psychology of Criminal Conduct: Theory, Research and Practice.* Chichester: John Wiley.

Blom-Cooper, L., Hally, H. and Murphy, E. (1995) *The Falling Shadow: One Patient's Mental Health Care.* London: Duckworth.

Bottoms, A. (1977) 'Reflections on the Renaissance of Dangerousness', *Howard Journal*, 16 (2) 70-96

Brearley, C. P. (1982) *Risk and Social Work: Hazards and Helping.* London: Routledge and Kegan Paul.

Brooks, A. D. (1984) 'Defining the Dangerousness of the Mentally Ill: Involuntary Commitment', in Craft M., and Craft A. (eds.) *Mentally Abnormal Offenders.* London: Balliere Tindall.

Brown, S. L. and Forth, A. E. (1997) 'Psychopathy and sexual assault: Static risk factors, emotional precursors, and rapist subtypes', *Journal of Consulting and Clinical Psychology*, 65: 848-857.

Browne, K. and Howells, K. (1996) 'Violent Offenders', in Hollin, C. R. (ed.) *Working with Offenders: Psychological Practice in Offender Rehabilitation.* Chichester: John Wiley and Sons.

Burgess, E. W. (1936) 'Protecting the public by parole and parole prediction', *Journal of Criminal Law and Criminology*, 27, 491-502. As reprinted in Cottrell, Jr., L. S. Junter, A. and Short, Jr., J. F. (eds) (1973) Ernest W. Burgess on Community, Family, and Delinquency. Chicago: University of Chicago Press.

Bush, J. (1995) 'Teaching Self-risk Management to Violent Offenders', in McGuire J. (ed), *What Works: Reducing Reoffending: Guidelines from Research and Practice*, Chichester: John Wiley and sons: 139-154.

Butler Committee, Home Office and Department of Health and Social Security (1975), *Committee on Mentally Abnormal Offenders.* Cm 6244. London: HMSO.

Butler-Schloss (Lord) (1988) *Report of the Committee of Inquiry into Child Sexual Abuse in Cleveland 1987*. Presented to the Secretary of State for Social Services by the Right Honourable Lord Butler-Schloss DBE, Cm 412. London: HMSO.

Carroll, J. S. (1977) 'Judgements of recidivism: conflicts between clinical strategies and base-rate information', *Law and Human Behaviour*, 1 (2) 191-198.

Carson, D. (1996) 'Risking Legal Repercussions' in Kemshall, H. and Pritchard, J. (eds) *Good Practice in Risk Assessment and Risk Management* (vol 1), London: Jessica Kingsley Publishers: 3-12.

Cobley, C. (1997) 'Keeping track of sex offenders: part one of the Sex Offenders Act', *The Modern Law Review*, 60 (5) 690-699.

Combs, B. and Slovic, P. (1979) 'Causes of Death: Biased Newspaper Coverage and Biased Judgements', *Journalism Quarterly*, 56, 837-843.

Connelly, C. and Williamson, S. (2000) *Review of the Research Literature on Serious Violent and Sexual Offenders*. Crime and Criminal Justice Research Findings No. 46. Edinburgh: Scottish Executive Central Research Unit.

Cooke, D. J. (1998) 'Psychopathy across cultures', in Cooke, D. J., Forth, A. E and Hare, R. D. (eds.) *Psychopathy: Theory, research, and implications for society*. Dordrecht: Kluwer 13-45.

Cooke, D. J. (2000) Current Risk Assessment Instruments. Annex 6 in Lord MacLean, *A Report of the Committee on Serious Violent and Sexual Offenders*. Edinburgh: Scottish Executive: 151-158.

Cooke, D. J., Forth, A. E. and Hare, R. D. (eds.) (1998) *Psychopathy: Theory, research and implications for society*. Dordrecht: Kluwer.

Cooke, D. J. and Mitchie, C. (1999) 'Psychopathy across cultures: North America and Scotland compared', *Journal of Abnormal Psychology*, 108: 58-68.

Copas, J. (1995) *Some Comments on Meta-analysis*. Warwick: Department of Statistics, University of Warwick.

Dingwall, R. (1989) 'Some problems about predicting child abuse and neglect', in Stevenson, O. (ed.) *Child Abuse: Public Policy and Professional Practice*. Hemel Hempstead: Harvester Wheatsheaf: 28-53.

Ditchfield, J. (1997) 'Actuarial Prediction and Risk Assessment', *Prison Service Journal*, 113, 8-13.

Dobash, R. P., Dobash, R. E., Cavanagh, K and Lewis, R. (1999) 'A Research Evaluation of British Programmes for Violent Men', *Journal of Social Policy*, 28 (2) 205-233.

Douglas, K. S., Ogloff, J.R.P. , Nicholls, T.L. and Grant, I. (1999) 'Assessing Risk for Violence Among Psychiatric Patients: The HCR-20 Violence Risk Assessment Scheme and the Psychopathy Checklist: Screening Version', *Journal of Consulting and Clinical Psychology*, 67 (6) 917-930.

Douglas, M. (1992) *Risk and Blame*. London: Routledge.

Downey, R. (1996) 'Home Office tightens vice on child sex abusers', *Community Care*, 4-10 April, 8-9.

Dvoskin, J. A. and Steadman, H. J. (1994) 'Using intensive case management to reduce violence by mentally ill persons in the community', *Hospital and Community Psychiatry* 45 (7) 679-684.

Einhorn, H. J. (1986) 'Accepting error to make less error', *Journal of Personality Assessment*, 50 (3) 387-395.

Epperson, D.L., Kaul, J. D. and Hesselton, D. (1998 Oct.) *Final report of the development of the Minnesota Sex Offender Screening Tool-Revised (MnSOST-R)*. Presentation at the 17th Annual Research and Treatment Conference of the Association for the Treatment of Sexual Abusers, Vancouver, British Columbia.

Feeley, M. and Simon, J. (1994) 'Actuarial Justice: The Emerging New Criminal Law', in Nelken D. (ed.) *The Futures of Criminology*. London: Sage. 173-201.

Finkelhor, D. (1984) *Child Sexual Abuse: New Theory and Research*. New York: Free Press.

Finkelhor, D. (1994) 'The International Epidemiology of Child Sexual Abuse', *Child Abuse and Neglect* 18 (5) 409-417.

Fischoff, B. (1975) 'Hindsight = foresight: the effect of outcome knowledge on judgement under conditions of certainty', *Journal of Experimental Psychology: human Perception and Performance*, 1: 288-299.

Floud, J. and Young, W. (1981) *Dangerousness and Criminal Justice.* London: Heinemann.

Forth, A. E., Hart, S. D. and Hare, R. D. (1990) 'Assessment of psychopathy in male young offenders', *Psychological Assessment: A Journal of Consulting and Clinical Psychology,* 2: 342-344.

Furby, L., Weinrott, M. R. and Blackshaw, L. (1989) 'Sex offenders recidivism: A review', *Psychological Bulletin,* 105: 3-30.

Genders, E. and Morrison, S. (1996) 'When violence is the norm', in Walker, N. (ed.) *Dangerous People.* London: Blackstone Press.

Gendreau, P., Little, T. and Goggin, C. (1996) 'A meta-analysis of the predictors of adult offender recidivism', *Criminology,* 34, 575-607.

Glick, B. and Goldstein, H. P. (1987) 'Aggression replacement training', *Journal of Counselling and Development,* 65: 356-367.

Gottfredson, S. D. and Gottfredson D. M. (1993) 'The long-term predictive utility of the base expectancy score', *Howard Journal,* 32 (4) 276-290.

Green, J. (1997) *Risk and Misfortune: The Social Construction of Accidents.* London: UCL Press.

Grubin, D. (1998) *Sex Offending against Children: Understanding the Risk.* Police Research Series Paper 99, London: Home Office.

Grubin, D. (2000) *Risk Matrix 2000.* Paper presented at Risk Assessment and Management Police Conference, Cheltenham, October 19th and 20th October, Moat House Hotel.

Grubin, D. and Wingate, S. (1996) 'Sexual Offence Recidivism: Prediction versus Understanding', *Criminal Behaviour and Mental Health,* 6, 349-359.

Hagell, A. (1998) *Dangerous Care: Reviewing the risk to children from their carers.* London: Policy Studies Institute and the Bridge Child Care Trust.

Hall, G. C. N. (1995) 'Sexual offender recidivism revisited: A meta-analysis of recent treatment studies', *Journal of Consulting and Clinical Psychology,* 63: 802-809.

Hanlon, M. J., Larson, S. and Zacher, S. (1999) 'The Minnesota SOST and Sexual Reoffending in North Dakota: A Retrospective Study', *International Journal of Offender Therapy and Comparative Criminology*, 43 (1) 71-77.

Hanson, R. K. (1997) *The development of a brief actuarial risk scale for sexual offence recidivism.* User Report 1997-04. Ottawa: Department of Solicitor General of Canada.

Hanson, R. K. and Bussiere, M. T. (1998) 'Predicting relapse: a meta-analysis of sexual offender recidivism studies', *Journal of Consulting Clinical Psychology*, 66 (2) 348-362.

Hanson, R.K. and Thornton, D. M. (1999) *Static 99: Improving Actuarial Risk Assessments for Sex Offenders.* Ottawa: Public Works and Government Services Canada.

Hanson, R.K. and Thornton, D. M. (2000) 'Improving Risk Assessments for Sex Offenders: A Comparison of Three Actuarial Scales', *Law and Human Behaviour*, 24 (1) 119-136.

Hare, R. D. (1991) *The Hare Psychopathy Check-list Revised.* Toronto: Multi-Health Systems.

Hare, R. D. (1993) *Without Conscience: The Disturbing World of the Psychopaths Among Us.* New York: Pocket Books.

Hare, R. D. (1998) 'Psychopathy, affect, and behaviour', in Cooke, D. J. Forth, A. E. and Hare, R. D. (eds.) *Psychopathy: Theory, research and implications for society.* Dordrecht: Kluwer.

Hare, R. D. (2000) Presentation to 'Risk Assessment and Risk Management: Implications for the Prevention of Violence', conference 17-19 November, Vancouver, reproduced in Annex 4 of MacLean report, *A Report of the Committee on Serious Violent and Sexual Offenders.* Edinburgh: Scottish Executive: 134-135.

Hare, R. S. and Hart, S. D. (1993) 'Psychopathy, mental disorder, and crime', in Hodgins, S. (ed.) *Mental Disorder and Crime.* Newbury Part, California: Sage.

Hare, R. D. and Herve, H. (1999) *The Hare P-Scan.* Toronto, Ontario: Multi-Health Systems.

Harris, G. T., Rice, M. E. and Quinsey, V. L. (1993) 'Violent recidivism of mentally disordered offenders: The development of a statistical prediction instrument', *Criminal Justice and Behaviour*, 20: 387-397.

Harris, G. T., Rice, M. E. and Quinsey, V. L. (1994) 'Psycopathy as a taxon: evidence that psychopaths are a discrete class', *Journal of Consulting and Clinical Psychology*, 62: 387-397.

Hart, S. D. (1999) 'Assessing violence risk: thoughts and second thoughts. Violent offenders: Appraising and Managing Risk', *Contemporary Psychology*, 44: 6-8

Hart, S. D., Hare, R. D. and Forth, A. E. (1994) 'Psychopathy as a Risk Marker for Violence: Development and Validation of a Screening Version of the Revised Psychopathy Checklist', in Monahan, J. and Steadman, H. (eds.) *Violence and Mental Disorder: Developments in Risk Assessment.* Chicago: University of Chicago Press: 81-98.

Hebenton, B. and Thomas, T. (1996a) 'Tracking' Sex Offenders', *Howard Journal*, 35 (2) 97-112.

Hebenton, B. and Thomas, T. (1996b) 'Sex Offenders in the Community: Reflections of Problems of Law, Community and Risk Management in the U.S.A., England and Wales', *International Journal of Social Law*, 24 (4) 427.

Hebenton, B. and Thomas, T. (1997) *Keeping Track? Observations on Sex Offender Registers in the U.S.* Crime and Detection and Prevention Series Paper 83, London: Home Office, Police Research Group.

Hedderman, C. and Sugg, D. (1996) *Does treating sex offenders reduce re-offending?* Research Findings, No 45. Home Office Research and Statistics Directorate. London.

Her Majesty's Inspectorate of Probation (1998a) *A Guide to Effective Practice: Evidence Based Practice.* London: Home Office.

Her Majesty's Inspectorate of Probation (1998b) *Exercising constant vigilance: The Role of the Probation Service in Protecting the Public from Sex Offenders. Report of a Thematic Inspection.* London: Home Office.

Heyman, B. (1997) *Risk, Health and Health Care: A Qualitative Approach.* London: Edward Arnold.

Hollin, C. R. (1993) Contemporary psychological research into violence: an overview, in P. J. Taylor (ed.) *Violence in Society,* London: Royal College of Physicians, pp. 55-67.

Hollin, C. R. (1995) 'The meaning and implications of "Programme Integrity"', in McGuire J. (ed.) *What Works: Reducing Reoffending: Guidelines from Research and Practice.* Chichester: John Wiley. 195-208.

Home Office Circular (HOC 39/1997) *Sex Offenders Act 1997.* London: Home Office.

Home Office (1991) *Criminal Justice Act 1991* London: HMSO.

Home Office (1988) *The Registration and Review of Serious Offenders.* Home Office Letter to Chief Probation Officers.

Home Office (1996) *Protecting the Public: The Government's Strategy on Crime in England and Wales.* London: HMSO.

Home Office (1997a) *Community Protection Order - A Consultation Paper.* London: HMSO.

Home Office (1997b) *Management and Assessment of Risk in the Probation Service.* London: HMSO.

Home Office (1998a) *Aspects of Crime: Children as Victims 1996.* Compiled by the Crime and Criminal Justice Unit, Research and Statistics Directorate. London: Home Office.

Home Office (1998b) *The Crime and Disorder Act 1998. Introductory Guide.* London: Home Office.

Home Office (1999) *Managing Dangerous People with Severe Personality Disorder: Proposals for policy development,* London: Home Office.

Home Office (2000) 'Government proposals better to protect children from sex and violent offenders' Home Office News Release, 15 September 2000

Howells, K. (1989) 'Anger management methods in relation to the prevention of violent behaviour', in Archer, J. and Browne, K. D. (eds.) *Human Aggression Naturalistic Approaches.* London: Routledge: 182-216.

Howells, K. (1987) 'Forensic problems: investigation', in Lindsay, S., and Powell, C., (eds.), *A Handbook of Clinical Adult Psychology*. London: Gower.

Howells, K. and Hollin, C. R. (1989) *Clinical Approaches to Violence*. Chichester: John Wiley.

Kahneman, D. and Tversky, A. (1973) 'On the psychology of prediction', *Psychological Review*, 80, 237-251.

Kemshall, H. (1996a) *Reviewing Risk: A review of research on the assessment and management of risk and dangerousness: implications for policy and practice in the Probation Service*. A report for the Home Office Research and Statistics Directorate. London: Home Office.

Kemshall, H. (1996b) 'Offender Risk and Probation Practice', in Kemshall, H., and Pritchard, J. (eds.) *Good Practice in Risk Assessment and Risk Management*, volume 1. London: Jessica Kingsley Publications: 133-145.

Kemshall, H. (1997) 'The dangerous are always with us: dangerousness and the role of the probation service', VISTA, 2, (3) 136-153.

Kemshall, H. (1998a) *Risk in Probation Practice*. Aldershot: Ashgate.

Kemshall, H. (1998b) 'Defensible Decisions for Risk: Or "Its the Doers Wot Get the Blame"', *Probation Journal*, 45 (2) 67-72.

Klassen, C. (1999) Predicting Aggression in Psychiatric In-Patients Using 10 Historical Factors: Validating the 'H' of the HCR-20. Unpublished thesis, Vancouver: Simon Fraser University.

Laws, D. R. (1996) 'Relapse prevention or harm reduction', *Journal of Research and Treatment*, 8 (3) 243-247.

Limandri, B. J. and Sheridan, D. J. (1995) 'The prediction of intentional interpersonal violence: An introduction', inCampbell, J. (ed) *Assessing Dangerousness: Violence by Sexual Offenders, Batterers, and Child Abusers*. London: Sage: 1-19.

Lloyd, C., Mair, G. and Hough, M. (1994) *Explaining reconviction rates: a critical analysis*. Home Office Research and Planning Report, 136. London: HMSO.

London Borough of Brent (1985) **A Child in Trust: the Report of the Panel of Inquiry into the circumstances surrounding the death of Jasmine Beckford.** Presented to the Brent Borough Council and to the Brent Health Authority by members of the Panel of Inquiry. London Borough of Brent.

Losel, F. (1995) 'The efficacy of correctional treatment: A review and synthesis of meta-evaluations', in McGuire, J., (ed.) *What Works: Reducing Reoffending.* Chichester: John Wiley: 79-111.

MacLean Report (2000) *A report on the committee on Serious Violent and Sexual Offenders.* Edinburgh: Scottish Executive.

Mair, G. (1997) (ed.) *Evaluating the Effectiveness of Community Penalties.* Aldershot: Avebury:

Maguire, M., Kemshall, H., Noakes, L. and Wincup, E. (2001) *Risk management of sexual and violent offenders: The work of Public Protection Panels.* London: Home Office

Marshall, W. and Barbaree, H. E. (1990) 'An Integrated Theory of the Etiology of Sexual Offending', in Marshall, W. L., Laws, D. R and Barbaree, H. E.(eds.) *A Handbook of Sexual Assault.* New York: Plenum.

Marshall, W. L., Ward, T., Jones, R., Johnston, P. and Barbaree, H. E. (1991) 'An Optimistic Evaluation of the Treatment Outcome with Sex Offenders', *Violence Update,* 1 (7) 8-11.

Marshall, W. L., Anderson, D. and Fernandez, Y. (1999) *Cognitive Behavioural Treatment of Sexual Offenders.* Chichester: John Wiley.

Marshall, W. L. and Barbaree, H. E. (1988) 'The Long-Term Evaluation of a Behavioral Treatment Program for Child Molesters', *Behaviour, Research and Theory,* 26 (6) 499-511.

May, C. (1999) *Explaining reconviction following a community sentence: the role of social factors.* Home Office Research Study 192, London: Home Office.

McDermott, P. A., Alterman, A. I., Cacciola, J. S., Rutherford, M. J., Newman, J. P. and Mulholland, E. M. (2000) 'Generality of Psychopathy Checklist-Revised factors over prisoners and substance-dependent patients', *Journal of Clinical and Consulting Psychology,* 68: 181-186.

McEwan, S. and Sullivan, J. (1996) 'Sex Offender Risk Assessment', in Kemshall, H. and Pritchard, J. (eds) *Good Practice in Risk Assessment and Risk Management.* London: Jessica Kingsley Publishers: 146-158.

McGuire, J. (1997) 'A short introduction to meta-analysis', *VISTA*, 3, (3) 163-176.

McGuire, J. and Priestley, P. (1985) *Offending Behaviour: Skills and Stratagems for Going Straight.* London: Batsford.

McGuire, J. and Priestley, P. (1995) 'Reviewing 'What Works': Past, Present and Future', in McGuire, J. (ed.) *What Works: Reducing Reoffending: Guidelines from Research and Practice.* Chichester: John Wiley: 3-34.

McIvor, G. (1997) 'Evaluative research in probation: progress and prospects', in Mair, G., (ed.), *Evaluating the Effectiveness of Community Penalties.* Avebury: Aldershot: 1-18.

Megargee, E. (1976) 'The prediction of dangerous behaviour', *Criminal Justice and Behaviour*, 3: 3-21.

Menzies, R., Webster, C. D., McMain, S., Staley, S. and Scaglione, R. (1994) 'The dimensions of dangerousness revisited', *Law and Human Behaviour*, 18 (1) 1-20.

Milner, J. S. and Campbell, J. C. (1995) 'Prediction issues for practitioners', in Campbell, J. (ed.) *Assessing Dangerousness: Violence by Sexual Offenders, Batterers, and Child Abusers.* London: Sage: 41-67.

Monahan, J. (1981) *The Clinical Prediction of Violence.* Beverley Hills, CA: Sage.

Monahan, J. (1993) 'Limiting therapist exposure to Tarasoff liability: Guidelines for risk containment', *American Psychologist*, 48: 242-250.

Monahan, J., Steadman, H., Appelbaum, P., Robbins, P. C.,, Mulvey, E.P., Silver, E., Roth, L. H., and Grisso, T. (2000) 'Developing a clinically useful actuarial tool for assessing violence risk', *British Journal of Psychiatry*, 176: 312-319.

Moore, B. (1996) *Risk Assessment: A Practitioner's Guide to Predicting Harmful Behaviour.* London: Whiting and Birch.

Mossman, D. (1994) 'Assessing Predictions of Violence: Being Accurate about Accuracy', *Journal of Consulting and Clinical Psychology*, 62 (4) 783-792.

Nagayama-Hall, G. C. (1995) 'Sexual Offender Recidivism: A Meta-Analysis of Recent Treatment Studies', *Journal of Consulting and Clinical Psychology*, 63 (5) 802-809.

Nash, M. (1999) *Police, Probation and Protecting the Public*. London: Blackwell Press.

Nisbett, R., Borigda, E., Crandall, R. and Reed, H. (1976) 'Popular induction: Information is not necessarily informative', in Carroll, J. and Payne, J. (eds.) *Cognition and Social Behaviour*. Hillsdale, NJ: Erlbaum.

Parton, N. (1996) 'Social work, risk and the blaming system', in Parton, N. (ed.) *Social Theory, Social Change and Social Work*. London: Routledge: 98-114.

Plotnikoff, J. and Woolfson, R. (2000) *Where are they now? An evaluation of sex offender registration in England and Wales* London: Home Office.

Pollock, N., McBain, I. and Webster, C. D. (1989) 'Clinical decision making the assessment of dangerousness', in Howells, K. and Hollin, C. R. (eds.) *Clinical Approaches to Violence*. Chichester: John Wiley: 89-115.

Power, H. (1998) *Sex Offenders and the Crime and Disorder Act 1998*. Workshop at the Crime and Disorder Act Conference, The Scarman Centre, Leicester University, Leicester, 19th November 1998.

Power, H. (1999) 'The Crime and Disorder Act 1998: (1) Sex Offender, Privacy and the Police', *Criminal Law Review*: 3-16.

Prentky, R. A. (1995) 'A Rationale for the Treatment of Sex Offenders: Pro Bono Publico', inMcGuire, J. (ed.) *What Works: Reducing Reoffending-Guidelines from Research and Practice*. Chichester: John Wiley.

Prins, H. (1988) 'Dangerous Clients: Further Observations on the Limits of Mayhem', *British Journal of Social Work*: 18: 593-609.

Proctor, E. (1996) *Community Based Interventions with Sex Offenders Organised by the Probation Service: A Survey of Current Practice*. London: Association of Chief Probation Officers.

Quinsey, V. L., Harris, G. T., Rice, M. E. and Lalumiere, M. L. (1993) 'Assessing Treatment Efficacy in Outcome Studies of Sex Offenders', *Journal of Interpersonal Violence*, 8 (4) 512-523.

Quinsey, V. L., Rice, M. E. and Harris, G. T. (1995a) 'Actuarial prediction of sexual recidivism', *Journal of Interpersonal Violence*, 10, 85-103.

Quinsey, L., Lalumiere, M, L., Rice, M. E. and Harris, G. T. (1995b) 'Predicting Sexual Offences', in Campbell, J.C. (ed.): *Assessing Dangerousness: Violence by Sexual Offenders, Batterers, and Child Abusers.* London: Sage: 114-137.

Quinsey, L., Harris, G. T., Rice, M.E. and Cormier, C. A. (1998) *Violent Offenders: Appraising and Managing the Risk.* Washington D.C: American Psychological Association.

Raynor, P. (1997) *Implementing the 'Level of Service Inventory-Revised' (LSI-R) in Britain: Initial results from five probation areas.* Swansea: The Cognitive Centre Foundation.

Rice, M. E. (1997) 'Violent Offender Research and Implications for the Criminal Justice System', *American Psychologist*, 52 (4) 414-423.

Rice, M. E. and Harris, G. T. (1997) 'Cross-validation and extension of the Violence Risk Appraisal Guide for child molesters and rapists', *Law and Human Behaviour*, 21, 231-241.

Rice, M. E. and Harris, G. T. (1995) 'Violent recidivism: Assessing predictive validity', *Journal of Consulting and Clinical Psychology*, 63: 737-748.

Rice, M. E., Harris, G. T. and Cormier, C. A. (1992) 'An evaluation of a maximum security therapeutic community for psychopaths and other mentally disordered offenders', *Law and Human Behaviour*, 16: 399-412.

Risk Assessment and Management Police Conference, Cheltenham, October 19th and 20th, 2000, Moat House Hotel.

Ross, R. R. and Fabiano, E. A. (1985) *Time to Think: A Cognitive Model of Delinquency Prevention and Offender Rehabilitation.* Johnson City: Institute of Social Sciences and Arts.

Ryan, G., Lane, S., Davies, J. and Isaac. C. (1987) 'Juvenile sex offenders: development and correction', *Child Abuse and Neglect*, 11, 385-395.

REFERENCES

Ryan, T. (1996) 'Risk management and people with mental health problems', in Kemshall, H. and Pritchard, J. (eds.) *Good Practice in Risk Assessment and Risk Management*. London: Jessica Kingsley: 93-108.

Salter, A. (1988) *Child Sex Offenders and Victims*. London: Sage.

Scott, P. (1977) 'Assessing dangerousness in criminals', *British Journal of Psychiatry*, 131: 127-142.

Scottish Office Social Work Inspectorate (1997) *A Commitment to Protect. Supervising Sex Offenders: Proposals for More Effective Practice*. Edinburgh: Scottish Office.

Sentencing News (1998) 'New Legislation: The Crime and Disorder Act 1998': 8-12.

Shah, S. (1978) 'Dangerousness and mental illness. Some conceptual, prediction and policy dilemmas', in Frederick, C. (ed.), *Dangerous Behaviour: A Problem in Law and Mental Health*. NIMH DHEW Publications No (ADM) 78-563, Washington DC.:Supt. of Docs., Govt. Print Office 153-191.

Steadman, H. J., Monahan, J., Appelbaum, S. Grisso, T., Mulvey, E. P., Roth, L. H., Robbins, P. C. and Klassen, D. (1994) 'Designing a new generation of risk assessment research', in Monahan, J. and Steadman, H. J. (eds.) *Violence and Mental Disorder*. Chicago: University of Chicago Press: 297-318.

Steadman, H. J., Silver, E., Monahan, J. Appelbaum, P. S. Robbins, P. M. Mulvey, E. P., Grisso, T., Roth, L. H. and Banks, S. (1999) 'A classification tree approach to the development of actuarial violence risk assessment tools', *Law and Human Behaviour*, 24: 83-100.

Strand, S., Belfrage, H., Fransson, G. and Levander, S. (1999) 'Clinical and risk management factors in risk prediction of mentally disordered offenders-more important than historical data', *Legal and Criminological Psychology*, 4 (1) 67-76.

Swanson, J. W. and Holzer, C. (1990) 'Violence and the ECA data', *Hospital and Community Psychiatry*, 42: 79-80.

Teggin, V. (1998) 'Crime (Sentences) Act 1997'. *Legal Action*, June: 18-20.

Thornton, D. and Travers, R. (1991) *A longitudinal study of the criminal behaviour of convicted sex offenders.* Proceedings of the Prison Psychologists' Conference. HM Prison Service.

Vennard, J. and Hedderman, C. (1998) 'Effective interventions with offenders', in Goldblatt, P. and Lewis, C. (eds.) *Reducing offending: an assessment of research evidence on ways of dealing with offending behaviour.* Home Office Research Study 187, London: Home Office.

Walker, N. (1991) 'Dangerous Mistakes'. *British Journal of Psychiatry,* 158: pp. 752-757.

Waterhouse, L., Dobash, R. and Carnie, J. (1994) *Child Sexual Abusers.* Edinburgh: The Scottish Office Central Research Unit.

Webster, C. D., Douglas, K. S. Eaves, D. and Hart, S. D. (1997) HCR-20 *Assessing Risk for Violence, version 2,* Vancouver: Simon Fraser University, Mental Health, Law, and Policy Institute.

Webster, C. D., Eaves, D., Douglas, K. and Wintrup. A. (1995) *The HRC-20 Scheme: The Assessment of Dangerousness and Risk.* Vancouver: Simon Fraser University.

Webster, C. D., Harris, G. T., Rice, M. E., Cormier, C. and Quinsey, V. L. (1994) *The Violence Prediction Scheme: Assessing Dangerousness in High Risk Men.* Toronto: Centre for Criminology: University of Toronto.

Weist, J. (1981) 'Treatment of violent offenders', *Clinical Social Work Journal,* 9 (4) 271-281.

Wintrup, A. (1996) *Assessing Risk of Violence in Mentally Disordered Offenders with the HCR-20.* Vancouver: Simon Fraser University.

Wolf, S. (1984) *A Multifactor Model of Deviant Sexuality,* paper presented at 3rd International conference on Victimology, Lisbon.

RECENT POLICING AND REDUCING CRIME UNIT PUBLICATIONS:

Policing and Reducing Crime Unit
Police Research Series papers

126. **Where Are They Now? An evaluation of sex offender registration in England and Wales.** Joyce Plotnikoff and Richard Woolfson. 2000.

127. **The Impact of Stops and Searches on Crime and the Community.** Joel Miller, Nick Bland and Paul Quinton. 2000.

128. **Upping the PACE? An evaluation of the recommendations of the Stephen Lawrence Inquiry on stops and searches.** Nick Bland, Joel Miller and Paul Quinton. 2000.

129. **The Views of the Public on Stops and Searches.** Vanessa Stone and Nick Pettigrew. 2000.

130. **Police Stops, Decision-making and Practice.** Paul Quinton, Nick Bland and Joel Miller. 2000.

131. **Profiling Populations Available for Stops and Searches.** MVA and Joel Miller. 2000.

132. **Managing the Use and Impact of Searches: A review of force interventions.** Nick Bland, Joel Miller and Paul Quinton. 2000.

133. **Serving Up: The impact of low-level police enforcement on drug markets.** Tiggey May, Alex Harocopos, Paul J. Turnbull and Michael Hough. 2000.

134. **For Love or Money: Pimps and the management of sex work.** Tiggey May, Alex Harocopos and Michael Hough. 2000.

135. **Reading between the Lines: An evaluation of the Scientific Content Analysis technique (SCAN).** Nicky Smith. 2001.

136. **Attitudes of People from Minority Ethnic Communities towards a Career in the Police Service.** Vanessa Stone and Rachel Tuffin. 2000.

137. **Assessing the Police Use of Decoy Vehicles.** Joanna Sallybanks. 2001.

138. **Widening Access: Improving police relations with hard to reach groups.** Trevor Jones and Tim Newburn. 2001.

Crime Reduction Research Series papers

3. **Alcohol and Crime: Taking stock.** Ann Deehan. 1999.

4. (Awaiting publication) However, 12 briefing notes under the general title **Reducing Domestic Violence ... What works?** have been published in advance of this publication. 2000.

5. **RV Snapshot: UK policing and repeat victimisation**. Graham Farrell, Alan Edmunds, Louise Hobbs and Gloria Laycock. 2000.

6. **Not Rocket Science? Problem-solving and crime reduction**. Tim Read and Nick Tilley. 2000.